No Talking in the Lavatory

Recollections of Parochial Growing Pains

by
TOM HARMON

illustrated by
JACK LINDSTROM

First Published, April, 1983

ISBN: 0-9610276-0-6

First Edition
1 2 3 4 5 6 7 8 9 10

Printed in the United States of America

preface

The following is a chronicle of attendance at Catholic schools in the late forties and early fifties—at the point in time when the Catholic school system was at its peak in the midwestern U.S. Shortly thereafter it began, at least in terms of numbers of students and numbers of schools, to decline.

I went through it so I'm telling it the way I remember it. The good and the pleasant with the bad and the not so pleasant. The Catholic school syndrome requires a chronicle from someone who was there.

It is a great sadness to me that so little is known about the men (brothers and priests) and women (nuns) who made this era what it was. To a greater extent than nuns, priests and brothers had an identity that went beyond just a name they had taken when they entered the religious community. They mixed with the secular world a little more than nuns and could be recognized as having human interests and personalities like other people. Nuns, on the other hand, lived in a tightly cloistered environment that kept them isolated from the rest of society. One could have a nun for a teacher for a school year or maybe even two and know nothing more about her than the name she went by, which of course gave no clues as to prior ties.

Nuns were rarely seen in public and when they were it was in groups of two or three or more and only during daylight hours. This separation spawned a morbid fear of what the rest of us had to think of as the real world. I'm sure that any nun alone in a public place in 1952 would have been frightened nearly to death. First of all, it was forbidden under pain of mortal sin. And secondly, her absolute unfamiliarity with secular society gave rise to monstrous fears of everything, but mortal sins mostly.

Who were these women and where did they grow up? They must have been a part of normal society for the first few years of their lives at least. In every sense of the phrase, they gave their lives to God. They had only the satisfaction of their work (teaching) and maybe a hobby such as sewing or music.

The structured life of a nun was such that she rarely talked with anyone outside her community. A nun's only contact with the outside world was through her students and some rare contact with the students' parents. All public places were off limits and, I assume, the restrictions applied to reading material and radio. (Television was just coming in then.)

A nun could go months without coming in contact with an adult male. Perhaps parents' night would bring some idle conversation with the fathers of a few of the students. And, I suspect the fathers were as afraid of the nuns as the nuns were of the fathers.

Money and other valuables were restricted. Money sent to a nun usually was given to the "Order." Indeed, the vows of poverty, chastity and obedience were hardly jeopardized. There wasn't opportunity.

While the nuns certainly missed the mainstream of life, they were undaunted in their service. What they had been instructed to teach and uphold they taught and upheld without reservations.

While this work isn't without some lighthearted jesting, it isn't meant to poke fun at the essentials of Holy Mother the Church but rather at the non-essentials. Any pointedness is not directed at those who participated in the administration of the Catholic school system but rather at the fact that the world the system prepared us for didn't exist when I got into it. Protestants weren't on every street corner ready to snatch our faith and Catholics really weren't discriminated against in the secular world.

On the positive side, a Catholic education did produce results in the area of the four Rs, religion, reading, 'riting and 'rithmetic. Physical harm would come to anyone in a Catholic school who didn't reach the required level. A Religious considered it a personal failure to have a class that didn't reach the national average on standardized tests.

While the following is intended to be humorous, it is also intended to be largely factual or at least based on fact. No real names—obviously—are used. The Catholic teaching contained herein has not been cleared with the "Imprimatur" or "Nihil Obstat" or whoever it is that's supposed to clear all genuine Catholic writings. This is intentional. What you're getting is what I got. If I didn't get it straight you won't either.

PART I

PART 1

chapter one

There—right in front of the urinals—the guy starts up a conversation. It could be about anything: "what a nice day, how are you?" Whatever.

It starts me to thinking. He couldn't be a Catholic. Not a "good" Catholic anyway. Because every "good" Catholic knows there's no talking in the lavatory.

The nuns drilled that in with a million other "dos" and "don'ts" through eight years of indoctrination that began and ended with silence in the lavatory. Maybe some of the brighter kids wondered: when did God say that? However, nobody was ever brave enough to ask. A lot of things were never asked.

From day one of first grade on the teacher was addressed "Yes, 'ster" or "No, 'ster" as the situation would make appropriate.

Everything was done in an orderly fashion and according to the "reward" system. When it came time to go to the lavatory—and everyone went at the assigned time whether he or she needed to or not—rows of kids were released. The best behaved row was released first progressing to the poorest behaved.

All with the admonition: NO TALKING IN THE LAVATORY."

I don't know if the nuns were born that way or whether they all had the same training manual. But of all the people of Catholic-school-upbringing that I've known the school stories vary little.

There are a lot of us out there in every line of work and we're hard to spot because we blend in. But to the last man or woman we don't talk in the lavatory.

Things have changed. There aren't nuns like there used to be and the ones there are aren't even called 'ster. Catholic school kids aren't privileged to have off a bunch of Holy Days the public school kids don't. Less than 30 years from the peak period of Catholic education, a generation of people, the last to be able to pass on the first-hand experience of a "real" Catholic education, are finding their memories of the old school days going faint.

I think it's time for some reinforcement of memories—a time for a chronicle, if only for historical purposes. It was too important a time to escape history.

The System

The Catholic school system was developed to provide Catholic kids with a genuinely Catholic education. However, it is reasonable to conclude from concerns that were passed on to the Catholic school kids that the system was born out of a perceived Protestant nature of the public schools. In the Midwest, the Catholic school system was complete from grade school through high school. Some systems included kindergarten, too. A kid started in kindergarten or first grade and went through high school. Catholic colleges were available, also, but attendance after high school was not necessarily obligatory unless the Catholic family had money.

The end of World War II marked the beginning of a huge expansion of the Catholic school system. Catholic grade schools and high schools were built in suburbs of the big cities in the late forties and early fifties. Prior to that, most Catholic schools—in fact, most public schools—were still located in the cities. In the late fifties, though, public schools were still growing, while Catholic school systems began to decline in enrollment and the building of new Catholic schools declined as well. Catholic parents paid heavily for the schools but whether it was something the parents wanted or something Church hierarchy wanted I was too young to know. This extensive system would never have been possible had it not been for the teaching Religious—nuns, brothers and priests—who served for very low pay or none at all. It is significant, I think, that many parishes had schools but only temporary churches. One parish in the vicinity had a basement church for nearly 30 years. The basement had been completed and made suitable as a temporary church with the intention of adding a permanent structure on the basement after the school was completed. The school was completed adjacent to the basement church but means weren't available to construct the permanent church until some 28 years after the school was erected.

The buildings were constructed and paid for at great financial sacrifice by Catholic parents. But the costs of operating the system would have been far greater—indeed, prohibitive—had it not been for the teaching Religious. Nuns taught in the grade schools and girls' high schools. Brothers and priests taught in the boys' high schools. Parish priests assisted in the teaching of religion in the grade schools. Grade schools were co-educational, so until ninth grade you had boys and girls together (you weren't supposed to notice). At ninth grade the split was made. There wasn't a coeducational Catholic high school in our area until the late sixties or early seventies.

Catholics had to attend Catholic schools. When Catholic schools were accessible, it was an obligation for Catholic parents to enroll their offspring. I don't remember chapter and verse but I accepted on faith that God ordered it that way. Indeed, the obligation was accepted without question by almost all Catholic parents. So if Catholic parents felt they could not send their kids to a Catholic school, they had to seek a dispensation from the parish priest.

The only theological concern was how far the obligation extended. Parents, obviously, were under pain of mortal sin to send their kids. Grandparents had some obligation in the event the parents didn't send their kids. And even aunts and uncles might feel the obligation. Certainly, grandparents should offer to ease the financial situation for the Catholic parents if finances were what was preventing the carrying out of the dictum. Aunts and uncles if of limited financial means might be obligated only to attempt to persuade the offending parents. Of course, if the aunts and uncles were of better financial means they might be obligated to offer financial help as well. And certainly the parish priest and other parishoners were obligated to do what they could to see that all Catholic kids attended Catholic schools.

One manifestation of this was the almost universally low tuition. Regular donations to the parish were, therefore, used to support the schools. This spread the cost across the entire congregation. There's reason to believe, too, that tuition might have varied a bit depending on the parents' financial resources.

Catholic schools tended to protect their students from the persecutions of the secular (generally interpreted to mean Protestant) world. Limited contact with non-Catholics was unavoidable, and to some extent, permissible. But the whole situation of contact with non-Catholics brought up hoards of theological questions. Some of them were: When is it permissible to see non-Catholics socially? Can one ever enter a non-Catholic church without committing sin? Is it ever permissible to attend a public school? What about contact with Catholics who don't send their kids to Catholic schools? And, my God, mixed marriages were a real theological dilemma.

Fortunately for us grade school kids, serious Catholic thinkers had resolved these issues and had the answers available. They were all in the Baltimore Catechism for us to memorize.

As I remember, and I did pretty well on some of the tests, non-Catholics of the same sex could be associated with socially, but not necessarily sought out, if no suitable Catholic were available. It was so easy to sin in this area that the only sure way to avoid mortal sin was to avoid contact with non-Catholics.

As for entering a non-Catholic church—never, never, never. In later years it was accepted that a Catholic could attend the funeral of a non-Catholic friend provided the friend had never been Catholic and provided the Catholic gave no visible sign of participating in the service. He or she might sit silently. No standing or singing because that would be participating.

Following the relaxation of the rule in regard to funerals, it became accepted practice to attend weddings of non-Catholic friends. It was, however, expressly prohibited to attend the wedding if either party was Catholic or had been Catholic or if either party had been married previously.

Mixed marriages, that is, marriages in which one partner was Catholic, were to be avoided by Catholics. If the two parties, the Catholic and the non-Catholic, stuck to their guns and insisted they were going to be married, a special dispensation could be arranged. But this was not done easily, quickly or without extensive pressure being put on the couple. If all attempts failed to dissuade the couple, the dispensation might be granted. We assumed that the request had to be written in Latin and be delivered to the Pope himself. If the non-Catholic partner agreed to raise all offspring as Catholic, not use any birth control methods, never say anything bad about the Catholic Church or its members and not be conspicuous about going to a different church than the kids, the pope would grant the request.

Now, as to contact with Catholics who didn't send their kids to Catholic schools: first, they were to be pitied and second they were to be avoided so as not to have the "badness" rub off on you. There was some discussion as to whether or not one could go to heaven if he/she didn't attend a Catholic school. As I recall, there was about equal division on this among the authorities.

By getting Catholic kids into Catholic schools for the first grade, the Church could be assured of getting most kids before too much damage was done. By that I mean, a controlled environment could keep certain things from coming up until it was time for them. In the area of concerning one's self with nuns, this worked in my case. I was well into my teens (maybe even older), before the realization hit me that nuns were really just women in disguise. When I was in grade school I don't remember being the least bit curious about whether nuns were women or not. I might have been a little slow, but the whole aura surrounding the nuns was calculated to obscure the fact that nuns were of a certain sex.

A Nun

I'll give you some examples of the enigma. Number one, the attire (habits) worn by nuns didn't give many clues. And names weren't much help either. Nuns were named Sister Harvey Joseph, Sister St. Anthony, Sister Thomas Marian and other names that tended to give a masculine connotation. (Considering my propensity for being on the receiving end of corporal punishment, I think names like Sister Joe Louis or Sister Rocky Marciano would have been more appropriate.) Looking back, the fact that most nuns had at least one female name should have been a clue. Sister Mary Margaret and Sister Elizabeth Anne were common as were names such as Sister Mary and Joseph, Sister Roger Rebecca and Sister Matthew Mathilda.

Also, nuns never went into lavatories except to collar a kid who was talking and they'd go into either the boys or the girls lavatory for that reason. Since nuns never used lavatories, or even ate in the presence of non-nuns, one couldn't even be sure that they had the same needs as the rest of us. This served to further obscure any identification of sex or even to establish whether or not they were really human.

Nuns never talked about human relatives either. They had their favorite saints and might talk about them at length but I never heard a nun talk about a mother, father, brother or sister. The cloistered life they led certainly fostered complete separation from the secular world. But they must have had families and some memories to go with them. I suspect many were separated from their families at a very early age, say 13 or 14, and therefore missed the normal family relationship of the teen years.

And I concluded, too, that their complete dedication might be questioned by the Mother Superior if there was talk about family.

If you had only words—no pictures—to describe a real nun to someone who had never seen one, could you give that person an accurate image? Now there's a challenge. But for historical purposes here goes: Nuns were almost entirely covered by black, flowing cloth. Some white cloth (and cardboard) was visible, too. Human shape was not detectable beneath the layers of cloth. This was planned, I'm sure. Nuns were really women like your mother, sister or wife but you'd never have suspected that from seeing one. I just figured God made men, women and nuns. Come to think of it, though, you never heard families talking about having a baby nun. They must have been born full grown.

In retrospect, had I been a little sharper, the generally high-pitched voices would have been a good clue that nuns were really women. But that was about the only real clue you had. You didn't see much flesh or shape.

Nuns were never seen eating, though at our school, they were brought lunch in a big lunch basket. A kid was dispatched daily to the convent to bring lunch to the teaching nuns. The courier did not observe the nuns opening the basket nor was he allowed into the room more than a few feet. Then, when the nun had properly received the basket, the courier was quickly dismissed.

From the top down nuns looked like this: A face peeked out of a white binding. Only the face from forehead to chin and left cheek to right cheek showed. No ears or hair were ever visible. Sure, the kids used to spread rumors that nuns were bald, but nobody could ever prove it. The cloth that covered the upper forehead, ears and chin (it must have been wrapped sort of mummy style) was white. Over the white, was the black cloth so all that showed of the white was a little on the perimeter of the face.

The nuns we had wore head covering with an internal structure to it that made the top flat. Other religious orders of nuns had habits that let the natural shape of the top of the head show through. From the front, you would notice first the large oval-shaped white cardboard breastplate which extended from the neck to just above the waist. Indeed, the breastplate covered the nun almost like a bullet-proof vest. I don't know for sure what the breastplate was made of but it was stiff, almost cardboard-like. The breastplate, I concluded later in life, was to obscure any bust. Designers of nuns' habits were hung up on the possibility of exciting the impressional natives and so went to great extremes to make certain any semblance of a feminine form was hidden.

The rest of the attire was your basic black. And there was ample cloth so as to obscure any variations in shapes among nuns. Some were a little taller than others, but they all seemed to have about the same build.

Just below the breastplate, a crucifix hung. And there was a cinch-like binding at the waist. From the cinch was

"I JUST THOUGHT GOD CREATED MEN, WOMEN . . . AND NUNS."

hung a large rosary. The looped rosary affixed at the waist usually toward the left hip, hung below the knees. Indeed, this rosary was a godsend to a kid pursuing something forbidden. The rosary kept a nun from being absolutely silent. When a nun was really moving or even moving slowly the rosary would swing back and forth against the habit making sort of a whooshing noise. And every kid found out quickly that a whooshing noise means approaching admonition. Actually, that's putting it pretty mildly. Admonition usually took the form of a solid rap to the head. But if you had a few seconds to cover up you could avoid permanent injury. The whooshing sound wasn't always enough warning for everybody. Perhaps a kid who was harboring an impure thought might be concentrating too deeply to notice it. Nevertheless, the whooshing noise was there for those alert enough to take advantage of it.

The flowing black habit extended to the ankles. Indeed, almost to the floor. You could sometimes get a glimpse of a nun's high-top black shoes, for example, when a nun was in certain seated or stretching positions or when she was moving to catch a miscreant, perhaps a lavatory talker.

The wide sleeves came to the wrists so you could see a little more human flesh, hands anyway. The huge flowing robes didn't have any visible pockets but nuns were creative. They usually kept their handkerchiefs in their sleeves. But their pitchpipes, and every nun worth her salt had a little round pitchpipe, were kept hidden beneath their breastplate. Near as I can figure, there must have been a pocket or fold of cloth inside the breastplate.

Now the nuns never dawdled when they went in after their pitchpipes. They were quicker than pickpockets. I suppose that was to reduce the chance that kids would wonder about that hiding place.

In summary, if you saw a nun from the back you'd see all black. From the front you'd see mostly black and a little white. The white would be the breastplate and a little white cloth around the face. The only flesh you'd see would be the face and hands.

Probably because so little of them was visible, nuns were ageless. In reality you could tell the older from the younger by the gait, sometimes by her quavering voice, but, most reliably, the force of her rap on the back of your head.

Even the oldest nuns worked, usually as librarians or hall monitors or maybe attendance monitors. Sometimes we were asked to pray for a seriously ill nun otherwise we'd never have known that they suffered from human frailties. It was natural enough to draw the conclusion that nuns were immortal.

Nuns Names

Nuns took their names at the time they took their vows, or sometime during the process of becoming a nun. I doubt that a nun ever retained the name given her by her family. Indeed, separating the nun from secular society was a primary objective of the process of making a nun. And families being secular society, the separation had to include her family. So a nun gave up her family name as well. Nuns never had last names. In recent years I've noticed obituaries in the newspaper that list last names for nuns (for example, Sister Mary Jo Smith). I'd assumed records of last names had been long since destroyed.

Nuns took their names from a list of their favorite saints. There were some popular favorites (as the cliche goes) such as Sister Mary and Joseph, Sister Mary Margaret (you will note that Mary worked in a lot), Sister St. Anthony and Sister Jude. Names could be of either male or female saints. And once a nun took her name she had to learn all that she could about her saint. Nuns talked at length about their saints. Instead of birthdays, they celebrated their "feast" days. I think that was the birthday of their saint. A nun might be a little lenient on her feast day. But never with a student enjoying an impure thought. Nuns were death on impure thoughts. I don't know how they knew for sure. I think they became suspicious every time they saw somebody with a smile on his face.

Talk about a sixth sense. Nuns never admitted having eyes in the back of their heads, but I never heard one emphatically deny it either. They could be looking at the blackboard and detect an infraction taking place in the back of the room. Sometimes they could be out of the room and know that a kid was breaking some rule or another.

Home to the nuns was a convent near our school. It was a distance of about a city block from door to door so the nuns walked back and forth. I don't suppose the convent was as convenient for all grade schools but all nuns lived in a common facility. There were no small groups of nuns living in neighborhood houses as there are now.

A nun never left the convent except on a legitimate mission and only in the company of one or more other nuns. There were few legitimate missions. Back and forth to the grade school was a legitimate mission. Maybe a few times during the year a nun might be allowed to shop for some personal articles at a nearby shopping center but I'm sure records were kept such that any nun abusing this privilege, for example, by asking for two or three trips a year, would be quickly found out. Once in a while a nun might be permitted to visit her family, her parents, anyway, if they weren't "fallen away" (that is, not practicing all of the laws of Catholicism). Brothers and sisters might be sources of scandal to the nun in cases where the brothers or sisters were not following church laws to the letter. So it was just better if nuns confined their visiting to aging relatives who were on their death bed.

Nuns were never particularly troubled by death. They didn't pray for someone not to die. They prayed instead for a happy death. I figure they must not have been all that happy with what was going on. They didn't seem to mind going to their eternal reward.

chapter two

At six years of age, school is something you've only heard about. But what was generally told to the younger kids as enough to instill fear in the hearts of the bravest. And I wasn't among the bravest so I was plenty scared.

How we got to the correct room for the first day of first grade I don't remember. I suppose when your parents signed you up you were assigned a room number and that number would be pinned to your shirt so the nun processing newcomers could keep everybody headed in the right direction.

When you got to your classroom the teaching nun took over. We had Sister Mary Magdaline St. Arnold. Because nuns take the names of their favorite saints, it's a safe assumption that this nun was attracted to Mary Magdeline and St. Arnold, patron saint of heavyweight boxing champions. The reason for her attraction to the latter soon became obvious.

She ran a tight ship. Later I learned that nearly all nuns ran a tight ship. No talking anywhere took care of most everything. The only time one was permitted to talk was when the nun directed a question specifically to you. Usually only a few words were required. Typically, a simple "yes, 'ster" or "no, 'ster" (as appropriate) was sufficient.

Because nuns had only the emotions of anger, hatred, revenge and, occasionally, reverence, their facial expressions were limited to the unpleasant. For example, scowls, grimaces, deep-furrowed frowns, and those you might find on a karate participant. However, upon meeting a parent, such as on the first day of school, even the meanest nun with scabby knuckles smiled. This misled the new students and often shocked the more experienced pupils who might observe it. By keeping the smiles of short duration the nuns could limit the possibility of it becoming a habit, which, of course, was a mortal sin.

It was common knowledge that nuns answered only to Mother Superior and God so there was no particular reason that a nun should feel obligated to be friendly toward parents. In general, I think the nuns tried to win over the parents so that when the nun requested additional punishment from the parents that it would be meted out without question. It wasn't uncommon for nuns to send home notes—sometimes with the miscreant himself, but often with a brother or sister—notifying the parents that the pupil had misbehaved and should be bound to a chair every night for a week.

It was, though, understood that parents had no business in the schools. Their presence served only to impede the process of providing a good Catholic education to their offspring. So parents confined their visits to the principal's office and that only when absolutely necessary. There was an occasional parents night but no PTA (Parent—Teachers Association) as was common for the public schools.

Once you were assigned a desk it was mandatory that you maintain its mint condition. It was clean, neat and generally free of other defects and imperfections. And that was the way God wanted it to stay. Messy desk, messy mind was one association to be made. And another was "cleanliness is next to Godliness," another Catholic tenet. I never saw it happen, but it was rumored that a kid could be flunked for a messy desk. It was no secret that part of your grade was dependent upon keeping a neat and orderly desk.

For the first grade, at which point the nun had no history on the pupil, the nun had to make seating assignments based on limited information. If you had an older brother or sister you would probably be assigned a seat based on your kin's behavior. If he or she was an angel you might get a seat toward the rear of the room. Of course, if the opposite were true, you'd probably be assigned a seat right under 'ster's nose. That was really what the system was for. Kids were seated according to how frequently the nun believed she'd have to discipline you.

From the second grade onward you carried your seating history with you. It was passed on from teacher to teacher perhaps by indelible marks. But for the first grade the nun sometimes had to make decisions based on first impressions. Fortunately, nuns had a good "gut feel" for troublemakers. If you looked damned scared you might get a rearward seat, that is, if you didn't look so scared that you'd wet your pants, in which case you'd probably get a front row seat.

Seating assignments weren't permanent so there weren't any really serious consequences in cases of slight misjudgment. A kid could be moved forward at the slightest infraction. If you didn't get into any trouble you would tend to slide rearward as the miscreants were found and moved forward. Several weeks into the school year, the talkers were all safely arranged directly in front of the nun and the scaredy cats were on the perimeter. This process was repeated each year through the eighth grade but for the second through last years the nun had history on each pupil so the shakedown, or correcting process, was much shorter. I'm sure the nuns prided themselves, indeed, might have had a friendly little wager for the best record, in not having to make re-assignments. The fewer re-assignments the better the nun was at judging.

Uniforms were mandatory at all Catholic grade schools. The only reason I remember hearing in defense of the rule was that it prevented "clothes competition." It was alleged that the students, especially the girls, would engage in competition as to which students could dress the most extravagantly and exclusively. Since the mandatory uniform rule was never relaxed, no test of this hypothesis took place while I was around.

"KIDS WERE SEATED ACCORDING TO HOW FREQUENTLY THE NUN
BELIEVED SHE'D HAVE TO DISCIPLINE YOU."

Uniforms did promote conformity and perhaps benefitted some clothing manufacturers. Uniforms worn by the girls were white blouses, navy blue jumpers and leather shoes. At our school, boys wore dress pants, sport shirts and leather shoes. Jeans and tennis shoes weren't as "big" then anyway.

But at most Catholic grade schools, the boys wore uniforms. The boys uniform consisted of tweedoroy slacks and a color coordinated shirt. Some schools chose blue combinations and a few had a green combination.

There was no acceptable excuse for appearing at school out of uniform. Even if you came from a family of nine kids and mother was sick in bed, somebody had better see to it that the kids had uniforms available.

In the boys high schools the dress code required dress pants, a shirt with a collar and "tie" shoes that could be shined, (therefore no tennis shoes). Without waiting for objections to be raised, the high school administrator advising us of the code would tell us that "if we didn't like it we could go to the public school." And, he added, if we thought it was bad now until a couple of years before the dress code mandated a tie.

The Grade School

Grade schools were large, classes were large, and turnover was low. Kids started in the first grade or, in some schools, kindergarten. Not all schools had a kindergarten so a Catholic kid might attend a public kindergarten and then go into first grade at, for example, Our Lady of Perpetual Penance Grade School. Kids popped out at the end of eighth grade, which was usually eight or more years after entering first grade. If, as a first grader, you believed the older kids you would think that the average sentence was about 12 years to get through eight grades. That, in reality, wasn't true. Few kids were failed and few were expelled. Move-ins and move-outs accounted for most turnover.

A class consisted of up to 50 "pupils," as the nuns called us. Had there been a movement back then to limit class sizes, and there was no such movement that I know of, the upper limit probably would have been 45 to 50. Classes in the middle to upper forties were common. It was generally believed, and results lent credence to the theory, that if all members of the class paid attention and diligently persevered, the limiting factor would be number of desks that would fit in the room.

Occasionally, there was a split class. As an example, half fifth graders and half sixth graders. The fifth graders would be on one side of the room and the sixth graders on the other. The nun would instruct one grade while the other would work on an assignment. It was sort of a throw-back to the one room schoolhouse era.

There was no changing of classrooms or changing of teachers during the day, or school year for that matter. Sister St. Rocky Marciano (or whomever) was your teacher start to finish for the school year. Occasionally, the priest might visit the room, but that was about it for strangers in the classroom. Except for a 15-minute recess in the morning, a 40-minute lunch and a 10-minute recess in the afternoon, everyone was together the entire day.

An eight-grade school of 400 kids could be staffed by

eight nuns, and typically was. Lay teachers (that is non-nuns) were rare. Usually grade school lay teachers were women, good Catholic women who might have had a yen to be a nun but perhaps fell into the married state at an early age. In eight grades a student usually wouldn't encounter more than one, possibly two, lay teachers.

The nuns handled routine relgion instruction, which has generally been thought of outside Catholic schools in an exaggerated proportion. Religion class might take up the amount of time equivalent to what was spent on any other subject such as geography, arithmetic or history. Certainly not more. But the presence of religion was never absent in any class on any subject.

Special religious instruction was handled by the parish priest or assistant if there was one. Usually, the priest's instruction was limited to a few visits a year to each classroom. Mostly it was in the area of testing what the students had learned. Since the priest was the closest thing to God that we were going to meet on this earth and because the nun herself might have felt a little "tested" by having her students grilled, preparation for the priest's coming was thorough and complete. It was often a let-down after a couple of weeks of intense preparation to have the kindly old priest ask a few easy questions, and then even excuse a dummy who didn't know an answer.

Nobody challenged the nun. "Ster, as she was addressed by all pupils, was the last word in all matters. A rap across the hands or head with a ruler, crucifix of the rosary worn by the nun, or a slap with her open hand, were the usual forms of physical punishment. And, of course, writing the multiplication tables over and over again was a typical punishment. Regardless of the punishment the nun meted out at school, she expected more to be heaped on at home if she sent to the parents a note indicating that the pupil had been disobedient.

If 'ster said somebody ought to work harder, there was no doubt about it. Perhaps that was one of the minor, or major, if you prefer, injustices of the system. Nuns had good memories and a good communication system among themselves. If a kid did something wrong in a morning class, by afternoon the entire group of nuns at the school knew about it. This was ostensibly so they could watch for potential evil and prevent the development of a hardened miscreant by punishing him or her before committing the misdeed became a habit.

And then the miscreant's act would be indelibly etched in the memories of all the nuns so as to be used as evidence that the pupil had had bad tendencies since way back when. Years later a talking in the lavatory infraction might be brought up to add weight to another infraction so the nun could invoke the "inveterate evildoer" syndrome. An inveterate evildoer could and should be punished more severely because the recurrence of misdeeds is evidence that the tendency toward evil is deeply ingrained and needs to be "punished out."

If a pupil were so unfortunate as to follow a high achieving brother or sister, the same was expected of the follower. And if the follower didn't come through, he or she was in for a special harassment. "Your sister or brother never got anything but an A," 'Ster might say "You should be doing the same. The only reason you're getting Bs and Cs is because you don't work hard enough. I want you to pray for the diligence to work harder and if you don't I'll have to take sterner action. I've been praying for you myself for months but you're an awfully difficult case, so I've asked that your cause be made our special intention of the month." That meant all the nuns would pray for you for a month. If that didn't work nothing would. "I know you can do better if you just use the brains that God gave you," she'd say. It was, and still is, a sin not to use all the brains that God gave you.

There was discipline in everything. Perhaps nothing was more pervasive than the discipline. Not always unusually harsh but always present and enforced. Silence was golden to the nuns. When in doubt keep your mouth shut. The recess periods and certain portions of the lunch period were times when conversation was permitted.

An example of this disciplined approach was the end of recess. When the first bell sounded to end recess, everyone stopped immediately in his or her tracks. And that meant immediately. Even if you were chasing a ground ball in a softball game, for instance, you stopped dead. If you were in the path of the ball and it hit you in a sensitive place you couldn't even legitimately grimace. Obviously everyone fell silent, too. For a period of 20-30 seconds, you had a school yard full of kids standing like stone statues.

Then the second bell rang. At that time everyone headed, silently, of course, and at a good walking speed, toward the nearest (but pre-assigned) entrance to the school. This was to be a bee-line course. No deviation was permitted except to those who might have previously been instructed to retrieve and return play equipment such as balls and bats.

Indeed, the very procedure for use of the playground was carefully thought out. Each class had its area of the grounds. This was to keep order and make monitoring possible. If a third grader were found to be in an area designated for fourth graders, he or she could immediately be taken to the principal where one was presumed to be guilty. I never heard of a kid successfully winning a "not guilty" verdict since the veracity of the witnessing student patrol was beyond question.

All trials in the principal's office were conducted in like manner to the Salem witch trials. By virtue of the fact that the accused was accused, he/she was guilty and the only thought given was to that of punishment. What would God consider a proper penance? No form of punishment was too severe, this was a "given." Only the opposite could be true. That is, it was possible for the punishment to be too light, in which case the principal would probably burn in hell for eternity. It might have seemed a bit contradictory to some pupils that a kind, loving God reasoned in such a way. However, any questioning as to the excessive severity of that punishment meant that the accused was not only an evil-doer, but a direspectful evil-doer, for which salvation, while still possible, was becoming increasingly improbable.

Only certain types of play activities were authorized and in certain circumstances running games might be proscribed. In the winter months "King of the Hill" was a favorite game played on the huge mounds of snow plowed up at the back of the playground. But this too was prohibited because of the potential injury to younger and smaller participants. In this game, the king of the hill was the kid who could stand on the peak and toss back anyone who attempted to take his perch.

By having assigned areas to recreate, it was possible to predetermine which entrance and exit a student used. Usually, the re-entry procedure included proceeding to the correct entrance and lining up with the other students in your room.

Typically, playground activity was monitored by students known as playground patrols. These were generally trustworthy individuals who could be counted on to seek out violators and report them. People with a bit of tenderness of the heart were immediately disqualified from this role because a monitor might have to "report" his brother, sister or best friend, a situation which might test the allegiance of the "softer" among us. Less serious infractions would be simply reported to the principal while serious violations might be cause to bodily remove the violator to the principal's office.

Monitors for the younger grades would be students a year or so older. This gave the monitor a physical advantage. In eighth grade the monitors would be of the same age so physical advantage could be guaranteed only by appointing the largest males to the role of monitor. And since the largest males were not always emotionally suited to the role, smaller but better emotionally suited would be appointed. This meant more "reporting" and less on-the-spot apprehension of violators.

Fire drills were conducted in the same disciplined manner. When the fire alarm sounded, everyone fell silent. All students stood up beside their desks and row by row the students were released to file out of the room. The path to safety was preassigned and the safepoint was a designated area a short distance from the school. The entire drill as made in absolute silence and at a safe and dignified speed.

Had there been a fire, we certainly would have found safety or at least have died quietly. A general, I'm sure, would have been proud of our ranks.

Ballpoint Pens And Other Evils

In the early fifties, ballpoint pens were just coming in. They were cheap but not as good as they are today. It was a universal fear among the nuns that these inferior writing instruments would take over the world eliminating fountain pens and good penmanship in their wake. Ink wells were still a standard in school desks, but they were not used for their intended purpose as fountain pens with self-contained ink reservoirs had previously obviated the need for them.

The elimination of fountain pens was a well founded fear, as it turns out, and the nuns themselves might have recognized that they were in a battle that even the Patron Saint of Lost Causes might have eschewed. But that didn't stop them from throwing the full weight of their influence into stopping the onslaught of ballpoints.

"A person should have a good fountain pen and be proud of it" was the credo. If you bought one of sufficient quality, say the $3 variety, it would last you the rest of your life.

So we all learned to write with fountain pens.

Fountain pens or not, however, more corporal punishment was dished out for poor penmanship than any other single disability. It was past the era of making lefthanders write with the "right" hand but the value of good penmanship was inviolate. It was thought by the nuns that poor penmanship was an impediment to success advocated by the devil himself.

So poor penmanship was not tolerated. You practiced, practiced, and practiced some more. And if your penmanship didn't meet standards, you were sent off to practice on your own until it did meet the standard.

Friezes

What's a frieze, you say. My, your memory must be short. A frieze is a decorative band around a wall. It's a funny, little used word though, isn't it? I haven't heard it since grade school. In those days, every room had a frieze. The area just above the chalkboard, a distance of about 24 inches between the ceiling and the top of the chalkboard, was well suited to use as a decorative band.

In most cases a frieze was a series of posters but sometimes it was a continuous sheet of paper. We all contributed to friezes and it was likely that one or more was produced by each class during the period of a school year. This took place mostly in the lower grades but extended into the area which might be considered junior high in today's terms.

I remember little about the subjects of the friezes (I have a foggy recollection that each frieze had a theme) except the sheer panic and fear associated with working on them. Any goof might ruin the entire frieze (or so I feared) and the punishment for that must be death. Anyway, it was mandatory that everyone take part, but not necessarily equally. Those better at it could participate more fully, which I certainly didn't resent.

Friezes were proudly displayed to be certain that the priest and, in some cases, the parents might see them.

In the low grades the pupils had to sit at their desks with their hands shaped like Christmas trees during music classes. It was a popular belief among the nuns that this practice enhanced musical concentration, if not ability. To do it right, you laid your hands flat on the desk, straightened your thumbs so they were approximately perpendicular to the fingers, touched the thumbs together at the tips, and then rotated the hands such that the first fingers touched at the tips. The result was that the area between the hands was roughly a triangle or Christmas-tree shaped.

Woe to the pupil who relaxed his Christmas tree during music class. Since everything had a reason and the reason for this practice was not obvious to me, I had to dig a little to come up with a valid reason for Christmas trees. As I see it, the practice promoted uniformity. Everyone had his or her hands occupied in the same way. This uniformity was aesthetically pleasing to the nun and it kept the nose picking to a minimum, something she probably also appreciated.

The Search For Contraband

The search for contraband appeared to be one of the few things nuns loved to do. And that was apparently because not only could they condemn you to hell on the spot (even a perfect confession cannot reverse such a condemnation) but they could pound you a bit around the head and shoulders while they were doing it. Corporal punishment is nearly a must for anyone caught with contraband.

Nuns rarely defined contraband. It was far easier to describe what was not contraband and let everything else fall in the prohibited category. But we all came to find out early that candy, bubble gum, baseball cards, marbles and other objects advocated by the devil were not to be coveted or possessed under pain of mortal sin. If a nun suspected that one was in possession of contraband she would immediately snatch the alleged offender by both wrists to prevent destruction or stashing of the goods. A person with a millisecond's notice would certainly swallow marbles, and paper or cardboard objects.

When the nun released her grip on the suspect's wrists she would warn him about any fast moves to the mouth (the Miranda ruling was years off at the time) and advise him to empty his pockets slowly. The smart offenders would try to soften up the nun by bringing forth first the rosary, then a medal or two and perhaps a crumpled up holy card. But sooner or later a marble or a baseball card would come out of the pocket. Few had the sophistication to claim the contraband had been planted on him by a Protestant kid. I think that one might have sold because the nuns worried greatly about the "walkers." Those were the kids who walked to school, often past the houses of Protestants who could be expected to do things like that.

Once the nun got the kid to cough up everything, it was immediately confiscated. Certainly one would be allowed to keep his rosary and medals but all else was taken by the nun.

A kid with a weakness for candy or gum could expect a long hard eight years of grade school. For sure, salvation was out of the question. I had a terrible weakness for the little wax candy with the sweet tasting fluid inside. I don't think they have it anymore but it was popular then. You bit the wax container open and tipped the fraction-of-an-ounce of fluid into your mouth for a second or two of rare pleasure and then you chewed the wax container like a piece of gum.

Of course I knew that these pleasures were temptations of the devil and that a person who succumbed to this temptation would be a sucker for the devil from then on. But it seemed so minor to me at the time.

I stored my candy in my desk and when we would change subjects the nun would instruct us to put away one text book and take out another. The desk tops opened upward, temporarily obscuring the nun's view of the pupil. If one dallied, as though putting away one text very carefully and neatly, he could withdraw a piece of wax candy and get it in his mouth while the desk top was up. With the right amount of practice one could accomplish the deed entirely within the time alloted to switch books. Provided one's mouth didn't move afterward, you could get away with it.

But the best laid plans can go wrong. A hot spell one spring got me. I opened the desk top and found sticky fluid all over the place. The wax had melted releasing the sweet tasting fluid to run among my text books and papers. Fear overcame me. I couldn't think straight. I had heard of criminals making it to South America but for a Catholic kid even that was not safe. There were nuns all over the world. I knew I didn't want to turn myself in. An early, untimely and painful death was not my wish.

I remember little of the moments after detection. God in his mercy provides "shock" to dull the senses. That I am still alive at all is itself an example of His compassion. Sister Primo Carnera, the teacher, and Sister Mary of the Rugged Cross, the principal, must have been fatigued from beating other kids that day. They must have discontinued beating me shortly after I lost consciousness, which was before I was touched. I've only fainted three times in my life, and that was one of them.

I was sentenced to clean erasers the rest of my life, to write "I will never eat candy" a million times and to eternal damnation.

Early in grade school, perhaps just into first grade, guardian angels were introduced. We were advised that everyone had one. Where they came from I don't know but it was obvious that there had to be one for every kid. That's a lot of guardian angels. Fortunately guardian angels don't take up any space. They can be on your shoulder or anywhere and you won't even notice. Exactly at what point they are assigned to a kid and just when they leave I don't remember.

All were highly regarded by the nuns, notwithstanding that a certain percentage of guardian angels must have been absolute and utter failures, if they can be judged by what became of those they guarded. I would suppose that even then the occupation of guardian angel was a precarious one. Today it must be an assignment the most optimistic of angels accepts reluctantly.

To the younger kids, the topic of guardian angels was exceptionally interesting. "Can I talk to him?" some would ask. Others would want to know, "Is he with me even in the bathroom?" Nuns were very patient explaining guardian angels. As I remember, guardian angels took up more time than almost any other individual topic in the early grades.

Offering Up

The subject of penance was never far removed. If one were subjected to pain or inconvenience, you could offer it up. That was the practice of enduring pain or inconvenience quietly and patiently for a specific intention.

If a kid made known to the nun via a scream of pain that he had just squeezed his finger in the desk-top hinge, she would very likely snap: "Offer it up for the good of the poor souls in purgatory."

So most kids got the impression quickly that a certain amount of pain is good. And that those who avoid it are really not very religious and perhaps have little interest in saving their immortal souls.

Now, almost any pain or inconvenience can be successfully offered up. All nuns counseled that pain from minor accidents should be offered up. I believe that pain from punishments is explicitly exempted from the category of being offerable, however. That is to avoid giving the poorer

"THERE WAS NO EXCUSE FOR BEING IN THE HALL."

behaved, such as the habitual miscreants among us, a better shot at going to heaven. You can understand easily the injustice to the generally well behaved if pain from punishment were offerable.

Multiplication tables were typical punishment for the middle and upper grades. If you broke a rule or failed to follow one, you spent your recesses and lunch hours writing the multiplication tables over and over again. A hundred times was punishment for a minor violation. A thousand times (the one-times-one through nine-times-nine) was the standard for somewhat more serious violations. Staying after school was typical punishment, too. Bus people, those who were transported to and from school via bus, were often exempted and were denied recesses and lunch periods instead. In the case of lunch periods, you were permitted to eat your lunch but instead of spending the remaining time in recreation you were confined indoors to do multiplication tables or some other type of punishment.

Throwing snowballs was an obvious violation. That cost me a couple hundred lunch hours and recesses one winter. A harmless black dog wandered across my path several yards in front of me, and for reasons known only to the devil himself, I picked up a hunk of frozen snow and hurled it at the mutt missing by a mile as I was prone to do in any endeavor that involved throwing. But I had been observed by one of the playground monitors (read "snitches") and was sentenced to a thousand repetitions of the multiplication tables to be written during recesses and lunch periods.

This use of the multiplication tables as punishment is

what makes Catholics today so good at simple multiplication problems. Catholics are the only ones that I know of who fought vigorously to keep low-cost, hand-held calculators out of the general market. We didn't need them. That was a battle that we lost, however. It's for the betterment of mankind, though, that calculators are so pervasive. So perhaps even God wasn't on our side in that battle.

Every Catholic grade school had a school choir and the nuns insisted on participation by all, at least in the lower grades. When the males voices began to change and crack in the middle of a note they were assigned other spiritually enhancing endeavors while the rest of the kids were at choir practice. Most males reached that point in the seventh or eighth grade and were therefore assigned to do math problems during choir practice. I never heard it said but I figured out for myself that the devil will have nothing to do with a person who perseveres at math.

When my turn came, the math problems turned out to be a lark. I think this lack of pain and misery wiped out the plenary indulgence that ordinarily went with this activity. The elderly nun assigned to guard us was sight impaired and hard of hearing. She didn't teach any regular classes anymore but still was used as a guard. I don't think she was expected to do anything more than keep order and "rat" on us to the regular teacher if we didn't follow orders.

Because of her impediments, there was a dull roar in the room at all times and a constant procession of guys heading to the pencil sharpener located near the door. Sharpening of one's pencil was an accepted activity and once one twisted the sharpener handle a time or two he could make a quick move, usually unnoticed by the elderly nun, and be out the door. This, however, was just a prank. It served no useful purpose because once outside the room it would be only a matter of milliseconds until another teacher or principal herself would pounce on you. Any break in the silence in the hall, and footsteps could easily be heard by the other teachers, would bring a nun into the hall on the fly. It would all happen so fast you'd not even notice the black streak. Nuns wore mostly black, you recognize, and therefore were easier to spot in daylight than at night.

There was no excuse for a pupil being in the hall so the capturing party knew the student to be an offender and quickly returned him, usually with a firm grip on the earlobe, to the classroom. Still, the challenge of breaking out of the classroom even for a few seconds was too much to pass up.

chapter three

Because many of the teachings in regard to sex have changed since I got my training, I hesitate to relate things which might have been superseded. But that's what life is all about, things being superseded.

Sex was introduced very late in grade school and it was never explained in great detail. Indeed, you really didn't have to know anything about it except the name. The tests never dealt with the subject in any great detail. Many of us knew it by name only for several years. It was generally believed at the time that things to do with sex could be picked up as you go along.

Fortunately, I've found that to be true in large part. As necessary, one can supplement actual experience by mailing for texts that arrive in plain brown wrappers.

Priests talked about sex. It was too sensitive a subject for nuns who were generally out of the room when sex was discussed. I assume the priests informed the nuns ahead of time that they were going to discuss sex so that the nun would know enough to leave the room after introducing the priest to the class. Nuns seemed awfully troubled by anything to do with sex. In their training I'm sure sex was not a required, or even permitted, subject. What a nun needed to know about sex she could get from Mother Superior or her confessor, whichever she might feel less comfortable with.

The topic of sex can be covered very quickly: it's good if you're married and bad if you're not. Really, that's all there is to it. You remember that and you've got a ticket to heaven.

Now, there always have been some deep thinkers who insist on going into the topic in greater depth. For them there is nothing but trouble. Because you find that when you go into a scholarly investigation, sex is really "good" only in very small doses and only as absolutely necessary. Now aren't you sorry I brought it up? It would be better if sex were limited to those occasions needed for procreation. I think it was thought by Catholic hierarchy back then that sex was engaged in entirely too much and that a lot less of it would be better for everybody. I find the older you get the closer this comes to truth anyway. I never heard it said, but my own unofficial statistics indicate that confession time could be cut in half if you stayed clear of sex.

Starting with the tenet that the celibate life is the ultimate in godliness, it doesn't take a person of great mental prowess to deduce that the "married" state, or "sex" state, if you prefer, is really somewhat subordinate. If you can't hack the celibate life, then the next best thing to do is get married. The way it was presented to us was that people were "called" to the religious life. Now if you weren't called to the religious life, or didn't hear the calling, which was thought to happen a lot, you were probably "called" (read relegated) to the married state. That really wasn't bad. That's all that some people were called to. You shouldn't look down on them but you can pity them a little.

Subliminally, I got the impression that you really didn't have to believe that sex was good at any time. If you wanted to be safe, you could believe that sex was bad all the time.

Because of the precarious perch on which sex is situated, many, if not most, sins had something to do with sex. Sure, adultry was covered but how many seventh graders had to worry about that? Fornication was thrown in the same pot and most of us really never had to know the difference.

For the safety of all of us, what adultry was or things like that were never asked on tests. The only questions in that area would be something such as: "Is adultry ever permissible?" or "is adultry always a mortal sin?" Since "NO" was the typical answer to questions involving religion the only concern you needed to have was for trickery in wording. Take for example the second question, "Is adultry always a mortal sin?" to which the answer is really "yes." Things like that could keep you from getting 100 percent on a test. Even the smart girls could occasionally mess up on a question like that. But it was probably better that you really didn't read questions like that too closely or dwell on them for too long anyway because "impure thoughts" could come even during a religion test.

Impure Thoughts

Now this is the ultimate position between a rock and a hard place. Impure thoughts are thoughts related to sex—always a mortal sin—and the type of thing that can take place without conscious action. Impure thoughts can occur any time, any place and they are always a mortal sin if you stop to enjoy them. And, God knows, a millisecond can go by so quickly that you can hardly tell if you've done everything humanly possible to get the thought out of your mind without enjoying it.

Now the spot is even worse because everyone is duty bound to avoid occasions of sin. And impure thoughts can arise out of almost everything, making almost any waking or sleeping circumstance an occasion of sin. Simply stated, that means that sleeping or being awake can be an occasion of sin. And you can't avoid both, so trouble is inevitable. The Catholic equivalent of Catch-22.

For adolescent age males impure thoughts can be confessed in powers of 10. Priests hearing confessions rarely gasped, but a week between confessions for a guy could result in a confession of 14 times 10 to the sixth impure thoughts. That could bring a long silence from the priest's confessional box. Anybody in that state was not doing enough to limit impure thoughts.

I quickly developed my own rule of thumb. Zero was an impossibility but a few hundred wasn't so bad. If impure thoughts could be expunged from the human existence, confessions and penances would be greatly reduced in length and frequency.

Now when you're in a box like that all you can do is minimize your losses. It takes years to come to grips with this problem so you're getting free advice that's worth millions.

First, confess a few less significant things accompanied by small numbers. If at all possible get a good rhythm going delineating basically venial sins, which are optionally confessed anyway. Then pick a spot to drop in 10,000 impure thoughts. If the priest has lost his concentration for a few seconds, you have it made. The litany of minor offenses is intended to lull the priest into a lax state. If you're good at it you can have him convinced that you're a three "Our Fathers" and three "Hail Marys" penitent and he'll be all set to blurt out your penance as soon as you've finished your litany.

If he picks up on the 10,000 impure thoughts, hope that he doesn't have a real hangup there. That could be good for a long sermon. Try to confess in round numbers. A very precise number (99,848) gives the impression that you are either very scrupulous or paying too much attention to them.

In some cases it might be a good idea to find out which priests have the lowest tolerance for impure thoughts and avoid going to confession to them.

What's really too bad here is that much of this advice will not help you if the church doesn't go back to the old way of confessing sins individually. I really don't have much hope of this because even the priests got sick of long lists of sins, so I've heard.

Somewhere along about the third or fourth grade, a nun told us about the INDEX—a list of forbidden books. I don't remember the subject being clarified much in later years so I know my knowledge of this subject is minimal. But that was all we needed to know. The INDEX contained books that only a priest could read. As I recall, even a nun couldn't read a book on the INDEX. This book will probably be put on it. Because I've never seen the INDEX I don't know what books are on it. I think even reading the INDEX was forbidden. Even then the sheer length of the thing caused me concern. The INDEX alone must have been volumes and today a complete INDEX must be a roomful of tomes.

We were told not to worry much about the INDEX. If we stuck to the books we were assigned to read, we'd be safe. And if in later years we were troubled, all we needed to do was look inside the front cover. You can usually do this safely, that is, without abridging the rule of not reading a book on the INDEX unless, of course, you knew that the book was on the INDEX and were just trying to stretch the rule and get a peek inside the cover. Inside the cover, if a book were not on the INDEX, you would find the nihil obstat and the imprimatur.

The nihil obstat (nothing objectional, in Latin) means that the book has been carefully reviewed by competent authority and found to contain nothing damaging to your faith. The imprimatur is like the stamp of approval from your local bishop.

I suspect the INDEX is growing by leaps and bounds. I certainly hope it has been computerized and perhaps put out on microfiche.

Indelible marks

Now we're getting into the heavy stuff but I'm better at indelible marks than I was on the INDEX. I remember being much more seriously concerned about indelible marks than the INDEX. I assume that if you need to clear your mind in readiness before getting into indelible marks that you have done so before proceeding with this part. There is one small problem. I had the flu or something during part of the discussion on indelible marks and so might not have everything down pat. But don't worry. It's close enough. If you are genuinely ignorant of something it's not a mortal sin. Just make sure you're genuinely ignorant and not faking it.

Indelible marks are invisible and unerasable. One each is impressed on your soul with each sacrament. That way God will recognize your soul from the poor soul who doesn't have any. These marks are intentionally generated as indelible so that no one can rob you of them. I assume that in the beginning these marks were issued in non-indelible fashion and Protestants rubbed them off some people. But this must have been a long time ago because as far back as I can remember they have been indelible.

Until recently, women had to have their heads covered in church. On the other side of the coin, men had to have their heads uncovered in church. But this correlated with the general rule of etiquette for men that hats were to be removed when entering a building, and therefore, the Church's rule for men wasn't a problem. But the rule for women was trouble. It extended to the youngest of girls. Any girl old enough to walk had to comply with the rule under pain of sin.

So you had the problem of grade school girls showing up for school on the day the class was scheduled to go to Mass without a head covering. Typically, a bandana served the purpose. It could be folded into a triangle laid over the head with one point over the back of the head and the other two points to be tied under the chin. While this type of attire would not be desirable in secular company (it might have looked especially out of place on a hot summer day), the piece of cloth could be folded and carried discreetly, used for its intended purpose and then refolded and tucked out of sight.

But trouble developed when a girl, or even an adult woman, forgot a head covering. Necessity being the mother of invention (I think it might have been a nun who came up with that) women and girls developed procedures to mitigate and prevent serious sin.

Like all other rules, the head covering rule required some creativity. If a girl or woman arrived at church for Mass only to discover that she had nothing to cover her head, sheer, unadulterated panic then prevailed. Nobody wanted to go through that. So the careful types carried a doily-like piece of cloth in their purses or on their persons at all times. These crocheted pieces, four to six inches square, came in black or white and were perceived by the Catholic masses as socially acceptable head covering for Mass.

However, one might be caught even without a doily. Nuns punished such girls severely. Remember that nuns had built in head coverings so they never had to worry about the rule. Lacking even a doily, a female might use a handkerchief, facial tissue (preferably unused) or some other piece of cloth in an emergency. It was generally determined before the class headed from the classroom to the church that all girls complied with the rule. And I assume all good Catholic families undertook a similar checkout procedure at home before leaving for Sunday Mass. There were some families who must have abridged this procedure because it was not uncommon on Sunday mornings to see a family clustered outside the church just as Mass was about to begin with mother madly churning the items in her purse to find a spare doily or hand-kerchief. Depending on the personalities of those involved, this procedure might be accompanied by loud whispering and strong words. It is, however, a more serious sin to let a daughter enter church without a head covering than to lose one's temper. You'll just have to believe me on that one. I attempted to double check in a Baltimore Catechism but I couldn't find the listing of sins in order of seriousness. I had long ago torn those pages out to carry with me.

Fortunately, the practice of covering one's head in church concluded several years ago. It was widely disseminated that the Church's hierarchy had, indeed, been caught napping. Apparently, somebody at a U.S. bishops' conference had made an utterance that was interpreted by the secular press as meaning that women no longer had to wear head coverings in church. By the time of this utterance the practice was somewhat less than universal and the tale of the comment at the bishop's conference spread like wildfire. Women in great numbers ceased covering their heads for Mass. The Church hierarchy went to some expense and trouble to dispell this ugly and untrue rumor (that women no longer had to cover their heads) only to find that women didn't respond by returning to head

"THE HEAD COVERING RULE REQUIRED SOME CREATIVITY."

covering. I'm not sure if the Church Law requiring women to cover their heads in church was ever officially wiped off the books. I know that some of the older and more conservative priests have been known to remark that is was not done away with. But these may be people who have not been in the practice of filing revisions to Church and Canon Law as they receive them and might, indeed, have out-of-date manuals. Jeans, tennis shoes, tube tops and worse may have provided a new front on which to wage battle allowing the "head covering" anomaly to drift into obscurity.

Oh my God, I wish I didn't have to touch the subject of birth control, but to be complete it must be discussed. To be correct, it is artifical birth control that is banned by HMC (Holy Mother Church). In the less complex and less troubled times of the pervasive Catholic school system, birth control was not a major problem. The grade school kids only needed to know that artificial birth control was forbidden. When it came time to know more we found out that we had rhythm, not good rhythm, though, because it didn't seem to work that well.

Families were large then and favored by the Church. When the church parish had a social event, be it a spaghetti dinner or whatever, there was always an adult's price, a children's price and a family price. The family price was generally equivalent to the cost of two adults and three or four kids. That meant that a family of eight or 10 would not be economically penalized. The practice of family pricing is still common in Catholic parishes but there is a much lower percentage of families in a position to take advantage of it.

Occasionally a non-blessed marriage would be ferreted out by Church authorities. This was usually something on the order of a man who had been briefly married while very young (perhaps to a non-Catholic woman) and then later married a Catholic woman. Let's say that the couple led a generally good life, produced a large number of children and seemed to be happy. Maybe this unblessed union had existed for 10-15 years.

Of course, the option of disolving this union would be very damaging to the offspring so Church law provided for the couple to remain together provided they lived as brother and sister. This option didn't seem to be used much, but it did exist.

Another situation was that of fallen away Catholics. These were people brought up as Catholics but no longer practicing. These people could be severely testing to other members of the family who, as good, practicing Catholics, were obligated under pain of sin to attempt to bring them back. This was in the same area as conversion and about as successful. The nuns gave us certain tricks to use. For instance, if fallen away Catholics were coming to visit, you could be just kneeling and saying your prayers as they arrived. That ought to cause a tinge of guilt in them. Or, at the very least, you could leave religious objects on the end tables or use Holy Cards of the Blessed Virgin Mary as place markers at the dinner table.

While I'm on the subject of old nuns' tales I should get some of the second-hand information off my chest. Nuns apparently were diligent about telling high school-age girls horror stories about being taken advantage of by males. I have to say "apparently" because these "tips" were never given in the presence of males, for obvious reasons. So this wisdom passed on in girls high schools where there would be no male ears.

Here are just a few:

If you are going to sit on a boy's lap, put a phone book (or other large tome) on his lap first. Definitely don't use the Baltimore Catechism. It is not thick enough and will not prevent transmittal of body heat for more than a few seconds. This is one of the very few situations in which the Baltimore Catechism will do you no good.

Don't wear patent leather shoes. The toe area is almost like a mirror. This is a very old bromide and almost certainly can be disregarded. I can't imagine that it would apply when the girl is wearing jeans.

If you have a boy over for dinner, don't use a white table cloth. It might remind him of a sheet on a bed and take his mind to the bedroom.

Don't (in fact, never, never) wear red. This is the color of passion.

Never take your feet off the floor. You can always rely on this one. No matter what is going on, if you keep your feet on the floor, you'll avoid serious trouble. If you think you're going to have a little trouble with this one, put a little double-sided tape on the toes of your shoes just before you think the trouble is going to begin. This will give you a little extra stick-to-it-iveness and it will give you a warning (slight snap) when you weaken and tend to pull your feet off the floor.

Nuns had great memories. Besides that, they had an exceptionally efficient information pipeline. This was not always an advantage to the slightly erring pupil. Since families were typically large, a kid might follow two or three brothers or sisters in a certain nun's class. So she'd remember the angel of an older sister. And you certainly paled in her memory. "Your sister was such a wonderful pupil," the nun might expound. "How can you be so terrible?"

If you followed in the footsteps of a miscreant, things were no better. The nun just naturally suspected you of everything that went wrong. "You're just like your brother," she'd say. "I think he still holds the record for impure thoughts."

If you had no older brothers or sisters, you still weren't home free. The nuns' pipeline perpetuated knowledge of any misdeed. "Oh, so you're the one who talked in the lavatory in the second grade," she'd recount. "Well, Master Harmon, you won't get by with that in my class."

The Three-Point Landing

Now, I'm not saying that a three-point landing is all bad. It is (or was) a matter of self preservation. Catholics had to kneel a lot and kneeling isn't all that comfortable under the best of circumstances. The circumstances in a Catholic church weren't always the best. You see, the kneelers weren't designed for human comfort but, instead, for human discomfort. This you could offer up. Adults, who were not inclined to "offer it up," developed their own remedy. This was the three-point landing.

Before I describe the three-point landing, though, I'll refresh your memory on the physical circumstances. For your knees, there were padded kneelers usually affixed to the pew ahead of you in such a way that they could be folded out of the way when folks passed out of the pew for communion and so that taller people would accidently knock down the one behind them when returning to a kneeling position. In kneeling position, the kneelers were about four inches off the floor and offered you a width of about five or six inches of padded surface on which to position your knees. Doesn't sound bad does it? However, the kneeler attached as it was to the pew ahead of you, was so far forward that with your knees on the kneeler you'd be leaning backwards about 10 degrees. That was the cumulative effect of the forward position at which the kneelers were attached and the slight angle of the pewback. This position required very strong back muscles and generally became a little painful even for the most pious.

So the older Catholics developed the three-point landing. You rest your sitting muscles on the pew (point one), your knees on the kneeler (point two) and your elbows or forearms on the pewback ahead of you (point three). In this way you were in a fairly comfortable yet semi-kneeling position. You'd have your knees on the kneeler but a large percentage of your weight on your sitting muscles supported by your pew and a small percentage of your weight on your elbows or forearms. Sure, it was a lazy man's kneeling position but it made those long kneeling sessions tolerable.

Grade school kids could only pray for the day when they could avail themselves of the comfort of the three-point landing. They certainly couldn't get away with it in the presence of a nun. Nun's were sticklers for proper kneeling posture. You didn't even dare take a chance on Sunday because a nun might be lurking near the back of the church or in the choir loft. It might not even be your teacher but she'd just love to get back to your teacher and inform on you.

chapter four

It is taught, or should I say, was taught at that time, that the age of reason is seven. I've heard no update to this thesis so I'm operating under the assumption, in genuine religious ignorance, that this dictum has not changed. What the age of reason means is that below the age of seven you don't know what you're doing so you can't sin. At seven you're supposed to know what you're doing. From that point on you're into sinning whether you like it or not.

From the age of reason on, you are obligated to obey all the rules of the nuns, other current rules of the Church and any that might be imposed in the future. All of this under the pain of sin. Don't get confused here. You might think that some sins actually feel good. That's just the devil fooling you. Sins are really painful—all of them.

Just to tickle the memory a little, reaching the age of reason meant confession, once a month if your family was just sort-of-pious, or once a week if you were either very pious or not at all pious. Kids were prepared for confession in first grade so the earliest of sins could be captured in memory and confessed. In those days, long lists of sins were rattled off which we'll get into later. Reaching the age of reason meant obligatory Mass on Sunday, no meat on Fridays, and fast and abstinence during lent.

Going to church on Sunday wasn't a particular problem to the one reaching the age of reason. Catholic families took the kids to church as soon as they came home from the hospital after birth so a seven-year-old was a veteran. Lenten rules weren't really a problem either because the whole family followed them anyway. In recent years the lenten fast and abstinence rules, greatly relaxed anyway, were modified such that people over 65 and under 14 didn't have to observe them. But I've never seen or heard of a senior citizen that actually took advantage of the loophole.

The obligation to attend Mass separated even the most pious non-Catholic from the least pious Catholic. When a Catholic vacationed, he, she or they searched out the Catholic church immediately, studied the sign posted in the church yard and made plans for Sunday attendance at Mass. I know of no other religious organization that requires its members to seek out a Sunday service, under pain of sin, when they are away from the local church.

This made arriving in a strange town on Saturday evening a bit of a struggle. After dark you might have to procure a light to read the sign in the church yard. Arriving in a strange town on Saturday evening usually went something like this: you stopped at filling stations until you found an attendant that could direct you to the Catholic Church. Then you drove to the church, shined your car headlights on the sign in the church yard, studied it for indicators of genuine Catholicism and, after Catholicism was established, determined the starting times for Mass the next morning.

First, on the subject of establishing that it was a genuine Catholic church, there were certain rudimentary signs. A genuine Catholic church would refer to Mass (not worship, for example) and the sign would probably have the "P" with the "X" through it, which is a common symbol used by Catholics. The sign would probably have mention of confession times. Names were generally not a good method of determining authenticity. Names overlapped heavily from one religion to another. In certain cases, one might use a name in the test for authenticity because such names as "Church of the Blessed Virgin Mary of Pagan Babies" and "Church of the Circumcision" just about had to be Catholic. If you couldn't be sure it was a genuine Catholic church from the sign you'd probably better check with some more filling station attendants.

In some cases you really couldn't be sure that it was the real thing until you were inside the next morning. But this was an awful risk to take because you, first of all, had to get out of there fast enough to avoid the sin of being in a non-Catholic church without good reason and, secondly, find the "true" Catholic church at which to properly fulfill your Sunday obligation.

Because you were probably on vacation and likely wanted to commit the least time necessary to obtaining the "full point," the result of attending a proper Mass, you tried to avoid the High Mass of the day. The High Mass could take twice the time of a low Mass. A High Mass in a small town might easily go 90 minutes, an eon when you're on vacation. Sometimes the High Mass was noted on the church yard sign, but not always. Typically, it was the last Mass of the day so you would make plans to attend an earlier Mass to reduce your chances of inadvertently hitting the High Mass. Indeed, if you arrived early enough on a Saturday evening there might be confessions going on. Then you could get into the church and perhaps read a church bulletin to get additional information. If there were confessionals and people lined up, you could be just about certain that it was a genuine Catholic church.

Attending a strange church during vacation had certain hazards for all members of the family. Besides the issue of time, the object being to attend the fastest Mass, there were other hazards. The father of the family had to decide what a reasonable contribution might be. Because the family was expected to make up any missed donations at the home church, the buck or two thrown in the out-of-town collection basket was in addition to the usual donation. Also, the family typically had to pack Sunday clothes for all members of the family because almost certainly if you showed up in casual wear that would be the Sunday the local priest would rant and rail about proper attire and you'd sit there feeling guilty the last half of Mass.

And for the kids there was the dread of the long, hot High Mass during vacation. A regular, or low Mass might take 45 minutes in the city. In the small towns it might be an hour. A High Mass in the city might go 75 minutes but in a small town with all the theological hoopla it might go 90 or more. So when you arrived in the church, you prayed devoutly for a low Mass.

"WHETHER HE WAS GOING TO LIGHT TWO OR THE DREADED SIX."

When the altar boy emerged from the sacristy to light the Mass candles you looked for signs as to whether he was going to light two or the dreaded six, an unmistakable sign of a High Mass. All a guy wanted to do was to get the full point in as little time as possible. I think the length of Masses in small towns is what caused me to form the opinion that the small-town Catholics were essentially more religious than their big city bretheren. The small town Catholics had to endure the long Masses every Sunday.

It did seem to be a common concern among the older priests, often stationed in small towns, that the congregation would go soft. God likes tough people best.

Indulgences

Indulgences seemed to be a greater concern outside the Catholic church than within. As grade school kids, we just accepted them. For the most part they were free or obtained easily enough. Who could take issue with a system like that? In recent years, indulgences have been de-emphasized. I hope they haven't been wiped out. Catholic school kids have chalked them up by the millions and to have them erased would be "horror" to those of us who are banking them, indeed, counting on them for our very salvation.

Almost anything non-obligatory carries an indulgence. Indulgences are typically specified in terms of days or weeks. Now to those who didn't listen carefully, the interpretation was that the indulgences were reductions in your term in purgatory. Purgatory is where you go immediately after death, to have your soul satisfactorily purged of evilness so that you can enter heaven. That is to say, if you racked up 300 years worth of indulgences that would be the amount of time reduced from your sentence in purgatory. I don't think serious thinkers ever advanced this notion. First of all, nobody knew anything about length of sentences in purgatory. The sharpest of Catholic theologians would beg the issue by saying that the stay in purgatory was just of sufficient length to purge you clean for heaven.

So indulgences were tied to earlier practices. The saying of a certain prayer, which, for example, might carry an indulgence of seven years, meant that the saying of that prayer was equal to wearing a hair shirt for seven years. In the early days of Christianity, people did penances, one of which was the wearing of hair shirts. You can imagine that wearing a hair shirt isn't very comfortable and this practice was a commendable penance. The bottom line for most non-obligatory prayers was the indulgence. A prudent person, of course, would look for prayers with the greatest indulgences. But this was never emphasized in grade school.

There was a category of indulgence, the plenary indulgence, which assured you of a direct trip to heaven—no stopover in purgatory—if you died in the "State of Grace." Every Catholic grade school kid had plenary indulgences by the hundreds. Even though, I might point out, that, in theory, one is all you can use. The easiest way to gain a plenary indulgence was to enter a church during 40-hours devotion. Because each parish had one annually, every Catholic grade school kid had ample opportunity to obtain plenary indulgences in great numbers. The 40-hours devotion usually started on Friday evening and concluded about noon on Sunday. During this period, one or more persons had to be in the church at all times.

You might have recognized that the requirement for gaining a plenary indulgence in the manner described did not include any minimum stay in the church. So it was standard practice to enter the church, kneel briefly in a rear pew, and get up and exit into the area just outside the church and repeat the procedure. One could gain perhaps 200 hundred plenary indulgences an hour this way. Some nuns approved of this practice and others didn't. Perhaps those who didn't were not so much objecting on theological grounds as practical grounds. You can imagine the chaos of scores of school kids going through this procedure simultaneously. The kids were bumping into each other coming and going and fighting over the rear pew.

Holy water was much more in favor in the early fifties than it is now. Non-Catholic acquaintances used to get a great kick out of telling us that the way to make holy water was to boil the devil out of it. Only priests made holy water and I never saw it done so I don't know if there's any boiling to the procedure.

Everybody had holy water. Special little bottles were sold during 40-hours devotion and at other times for the specific purpose of transporting and storing holy water. Grade school kids spent much time filling the bottles with holy water, splashing it on themselves, and refilling the bottle. Nuns approved of the use of holy water and the practice of using holy water was more wide spread then. Nowadays, it's used in special religious practices such as baptism and a few other situations.

Nuns were absolutely nuts about preserving things. It was considered an act equivalent almost to celibacy to use a pencil so conservatively as to make it last from first through eighth grade. I swear I could have done it had I been able to hang on to one that long. As it was, I rarely had any single pencil long enough to make it to the pencil sharpener. They're awfully easy to lose.

Keeping text books in good condition was a requirement of the highest priority. Any damage to a book would be punishable by death. As I recall, the books were the property of the school and were merely loaned to the students for use during the school year. By belonging to the school, the books ultimately belonged to God. And He didn't want anything to happen to any of His books.

So the nuns prescribed book covers. The procedure for covering the books was adequately demonstrated in class so that even the slowest of the slow could catch on. Damned if bringing the procedure to current memory isn't a little tough, though. What was that about the slowest of the slow? It was best if the book cover were made of oil cloth but certain heavy papers and other cloth materials might be acceptable if oil cloth were prohibitively expensive. Vinyl was still in the oil companies' laboratories then.

The book should be covered such that the entire exterior would be protected. The cover would be taped to itself inside the front and back covers so that no adhesive touched the book itself, just the covering material. That way a book was never marred. The student-applied cover could be removed without damage to the book.

Each and every text book was covered in that way by the student who used it. If one weren't very good at it in the first grade, an older brother or sister or maybe the student's mother might have to do it. Only the frightfully slow never mastered book covering. Unfortunately for the gifted, the requirement to cover all texts was relaxed in the upper grades and sometimes only the goody-goodies would be covering their books in the last couple of grades. It was a prudent thing to do, however, because it was good for a slight boost in the grade, say from a "D" to a "C," if you had your books covered.

Association with protestants was expressly forbidden under any circumstances and discouraged under all except one situation. And that was if a protestant should want to visit a Catholic church (read, potential convert). All efforts should be expended to see that his or her soul had a chance to be saved by seeing the true light.

Otherwise, even social contact was to be avoided for fear that such contact would lead to the desire to date, visit a Protestant church or, worst, to marry a Protestant. Dispensations (to marry a non-Catholic) were only occasionally granted, and, I'm certain, very reluctantly.

Catholic kids had their own schools, their own holy days, their own everything. That was to minimize the need to make contact with non-Catholics. Catholic newspapers and bulletins told you who the Catholic business people were, Catholic hospitals took care of you when you were sick. And the Knights of Columbus sold life insurance. So one could function completely without ever having to contact a non-Catholic.

Now all that discussion might make you think Catholics had it pretty bad. They certainly had to know a lot of things. But it certainly wasn't so bad you couldn't operate in good conscience. True ignorance was the loophole the Catholic hierarchy left for the masses.

Indeed, you didn't have to know everything. In fact, you didn't even have to suspect everything. That's why it didn't seem troublesome to pray to the Virgin Mary for years without knowing what a virgin was. Or to celebrate the circumcision of Christ without knowing what circumcision was.

All popes were Italian (it saved relocation expenses) and there were plenty of priests and nuns. The Baltimore catechism asked and answered all legitimate questions. If it wasn't in the catechism, not only wasn't it worth knowing, you didn't dare know it. Anything about religion that you knew that wasn't in the Baltimore catechism was almost certainly a mortal sin.

I always wondered why the catechism was named after a city in Maryland but the question wasn't in the book itself so I'm doomed to everlasting ignorance.

True ignorance—I mean, really not even suspecting— will protect you. If you didn't know what you were doing was wrong, truly didn't even think it might be wrong, then you really didn't commit the sin. If you had never heard of the Catholic Church and the requirement for belonging to it in order to find eternal salvation then you might be saved. Aha, see how cleverly I slipped that one in. Nobody who reads this book can, in good conscience, claim ignorance of that one now.

A kid who went through Catholic grade schools, so told the nuns, was going to have a damn hard time using the "ignorance loophole."

Still, ignorance can be safely claimed by many on some remote subjects. I have a feeling ignorance is used in far more cases than it really applies, though. The smarter kids bragged sometimes that they could use the "ignorance loophole" in regard to Legion of Decency movie ratings. If you weren't able to find the rating easily you'd just attend the movie and learn later that it was a "B," a movie for which the penalty for viewing it was a mortal sin. But, if you didn't know it was a "B" when you saw it, it wasn't really a sin for you.

Latin—The Language Of The Church

In those days, Latin was the language of the church. The Mass was said in Latin. A few readings/prayers were in English as was the sermon. There were no homilies then. Almost all devotions were conducted entirely in Latin. One exception was the rosary which was said in English. Almost all hymns were in Latin.

Still, as best I could observe, few people knew Latin. In the late forties and early fifties not all adults had come through Catholic schools so all the Latin they knew was what they picked up in church. Grade school kids were given a smattering of Latin learning but it was pretty limited. You just didn't teach a foreign language in grade school at that time, even if it was the official language of the Catholic church. Perhaps there were a few well educated people who knew Latin, but most people didn't. Everybody, however, knew what "Benny's Got all the dominoes" means. That, a rough approximation of what benidicamus domino sounds like to the untrained ear, means "the end." When the phrase was heard it meant the end of Mass.

One of the losses involved in the change to the vernacular, that's English for us, is that it reduced the mystery or mystic atmosphere. Mass, for example, just didn't have the same impact when the English words were used.

Even in the fifties people began to question the need for saying Mass in a foreign tongue. Indeed, Latin is a dead language. It is not spoken in any country in the world. But God liked it. If God had wanted the Mass to be said in English he probably would have made the U.S. the Holy Land. It was never clear to me at that time why the church hierarchy chose Rome over, say, London, Paris, New York or Chicago when they, the higher ups, were looking for a permanent location for the church's corporate headquarters. But I was never very good at geography.

Anyway, it was Italian popes and Latin.

Certain prayers when said outside of Mass were said in English. "Hail Mary full of Grapes" and "Our Father" are examples. But during Mass it was Latin. The Epistle, Gospel and Sermon were in English. The rest was Latin.

Because of the mysteriousness of the Mass, certain practices came into being, probably out of a lack of understanding. At least I don't remember being taught these things. It was felt by some lay people that even attendance at Mass, sometimes referred to as participation at Mass, though participation on the part of the congregation was at a minimum, could be improved upon by saying the rosary at the same time. Perhaps people even offered other prayers while the Mass was going on. This always seemed to me like a dilution of efforts and a depreciation of the sanctity of the Mass.

But the Mass in Latin was known and loved and not to be given up easily. It was easy enough to follow the Mass if you didn't have a missal. If you did have a missal, it was awful. First, all you saw was the back of the priest. He had his back to the congregation except when reading the English parts and when delivering the sermon. Many priests uttered the Latin at barely audible levels and the only way you could tell for sure how far along he was was to take heed of the few signs there were, the ringing of bells and movement of a large tome, the Mass book. Every so often most priests would boom out a latin sentence. If you were alert, you caught it and scrambled through the missal to find out how close to the end you were. The older you got, the wiser you got about the signs.

Attendance at Mass required a ritual of sitting, standing and kneeling at the proper times. It really hasn't changed much to this day but, if memory serves me correctly, there is a little less kneeling today. In the old days you gen- uflected as you entered the pew, knelt in the pew for a short time, and then sat until the Mass actually started. You stood briefly at the beginning of Mass, knelt for a spell, stood for the reading of the Gospel, sat for the sermon, knelt a while after that and then walked to the front of the church for communion. After communion you sat or knelt until the priest was through washing and wiping the dishes and then you stood for the rest of the Mass.

Because of this ritual, few Catholics had to worry about programs to stay in good physical condition. A devout Catholic got more regular exercise than a Major League baseball player.

Proper genuflecting was emphasized by the nuns. To genuflect, one bends the right leg to the point that the knee touches the floor. A good genuflection includes good, smooth movement, a light touching of the floor by the knee and a quick return to the standing position. Obviously, the curtsy-like genuflection in which one makes an almost bouncing like motion is not appropriate. This lazy genuflection, which often looks like the person is ducking a low-flying object, is almost wholly displeasing to God. For one thing, the knee dips only a few inches and never comes close to touching the floor. And, secondly, one completely misses the necessary physical inconvenience of returning your full body weight to a standing position. For this reason, a heavier person who properly genuflects gets more credit for genuflecting than a skinny person.

Though not generally recognized, the cloddish genuflection often practiced by the overly pious is also displeasing to God. In this type of genuflection, the person almost throws himself into the genuflecting position with full body weight coming to rest on the right knee. It usually requires a list to the starboard to get this one down right. On wood floors this is a noisy maneuver and it's almost always somewhat painful. It's entirely ungraceful in that it is usually completed by positioning one or both hands on the right leg just above the knee and pushing downward so as to facilitate return to a standing position. Sure, the person gets some attention from others when his or her knee pounds the wood floor loud enough to make a thud, but this maneuver really turns God off. He knows the person is doing it more for the attention than to comply with the rules. Moreover, to use the pushing movement to alleviate the inconvenience of standing up again negates the grace one might ordinarily gain from genuflecting.

All Catholic grade school kids practiced genuflecting until it was done correctly. A full grade might be deducted from your mark in religion class for failure to properly master the technique. Unfortunately, it came almost naturally to some who had little sympathy for those who had trouble with it. But the nuns persevered until all were at least minimally successful. It was thought that there were millions of people flirting with a destiny of eternity in hell for their inadequacy in the area of genuflecting.

chapter five

The missal, a relatively large book, was the tool you needed to follow the Mass—that is, if you could understand the thing. The Mass was divided into the Proper and the Ordinary. The Ordinary was the part that was said all the time. That part of the book got dog-eared pretty fast. That made it easy to find even without using the ribbons used for marking places. The Ordinary was typically located near the center of the missal. The Propers were located in other sections according to the church year which started with Advent, the preparation for Christmas. In the Proper you would find the specific readings for the Mass. Sunday Masses weren't hard to anticipate but on weekdays you never knew for sure whether it might be the "Second Mass of a Confessor Not a Bishop" or perhaps the "First Mass of a Virgin Martyr." It might even be a ferial day (a day on which there was no particular saint being honored or no special occasion being celebrated.) or the priest might have exercised his option to say his favorite Mass. This was an option he could use on certain days when the prescribed Mass wasn't a "biggie."

You had just enough ribbons in the missal to keep all the parts located. Between the sitting, standing and kneeling and the flipping about in the missal you were always busy.

It wasn't bad on Sunday. You could kind of flip the pages as you cared to. There was no nun around to check that you were in the right place at the right time and most of the adults weren't any better off. Sometimes a brother or sister might catch you being on the wrong page but snitching wasn't a great worry because parental punishment for being on the wrong page wasn't very severe. A parent might be on the wrong page, too.

But with the nuns it was a different story. To hear them tell it, half the people in Hell were there for not following Mass properly. The other half are there for obscene thoughts. You could get racked pretty good for being on the Gloria during the time of the Orate Fratres.

Nuns always knew precisely where the ribbons ought to be located and could tell from a distance of 50 feet if you had yours properly placed. It was because of this talent that one nun could adequately police an entire church full of kids.

Early on—about the first day of first grade—we were advised of the Church Law that mandates attendance at Mass on all Sundays and Holy Days. Most kids knew this before they got to grade school but it was too important a law not to emphasize from the start of school. I dubbed this the full point. You must get a full point on every Sunday or Holy Day or burn in Hell for eternity. There are guys upstairs (heaven) who murdered dozens of people but never missed Mass. On the other side of the coin there are guys downstairs (Hell) who never did anything wrong except missing a Mass or two. Not that missing Mass isn't a forgivable sin because, like all others, it is certainly forgivable but you never know when you're going to die. And, if you're in the habit of missing Mass occasionally, sure as Murphy's law you're going to die in a state of sin. So don't take any chances.

The definition of what constitues a full point is one of the most important definitions in Catholicism. So here goes:

A full point is accorded those who witness (actually, attend might be a better word but it isn't the official word) a complete Mass in person. The broadcast media do not count.

The tally in heaven is based on integers—only full points are counted. So do it right or don't do it at all. Failure to pick up a full point on a Sunday or Holy Day (there are some exceptions which I will take up shortly) results in a Mortal Sin. There is no way to make up a lost point. So don't go to Mass twice on a Sunday and hope to make up one you've missed. It doesn't work that way. Neither does going to Mass on a non-obligatory occasion make up for missing on an obligatory day. If you miss Mass on an obligatory day it's Confession or Hell—you pick it. Actually, I try to take a more compassionate stance on this than was taught in my day but my position doesn't necessarily correlate with that of Holy Mother the Church.

"SO YOU DON'T GO TO MASS TWICE ON A SUNDAY AND
HOPE TO MAKE UP ONE YOU'VE MISSED. IT DOESN'T WORK THAT WAY."

To get a full point a person must be inside the church. I think within sight of the altar is the minimum requirement. Unless an overflow crowd should prevent that in which case the closest you can get will meet the minimum "bodily presence" requirement. However, don't take this requirement too lightly. It isn't an easy requirement to mitigate. You are bound (under pain of Mortal Sin, I assume) to do a little pushing and shoving together of bodies so that all might get within sight of the altar.

Let your conscience be your guide here. But if you aren't at least a little tired from shoving and perspiring a little from the close company you might not have discharged your obligation properly.

In order to gain the full point you must fulfill the bodily presence requirement from the time the Apostles Creed is begun until sometime just after communion. I remember explicitly being tested on the "moment of arrival" requirement. All the nuns emphasized that one. Usually, it was stated, that while it was better to be there on time, if you arrived before the priest finished the sermon you were safe. Obviously, if you arrived later than that, you had better stay for the next Mass. If it were the last Mass of the day, you shouldn't have been so damned careless.

It was further pointed out that this fulfillment of the minimum was not wholly pleasing to God and was probably a venial sin but God has to have cut-offs, like everybody else, and so he established this one.

I don't remember as much discussion about the precise moment at which one could leave and still be assured of a full point. I've had to rely on logic to describe a cut-off that

I feel comfortable with. I deduced that it is permissible to leave right after communion.

I am sure that the reason this area was deliberately neglected by the teaching nuns was so as to discourage the practice of leaving early. But it only seems reasonable that if you have a minimum on the front-end you should have one on the back-end, too. Drawing on practices I observed, leaving right after communion seemed to be the right cut-off. I deduced that if it is legitimate to leave right after communion, then the non-communicants should be free to leave after the first person has received. And since the priest is the first to take communion, then this is the moment at which the Mass becomes complete. Don't take my word on this, though. The subject might have been covered in a class I missed.

The times at which a person might consider himself free of the obligation to attend Mass leave room for good judgment guided of course by good, scrupulous conscience. If you are genuinely sick—perhaps hospitalized and unable to move—you may be freed. A little sick isn't good enough. If you are going to get out of bed and watch television later in the day you are taking a chance relying on the "sick" loophole. Inability to get to the church might free you but this isn't an easy out either. A car that won't start isn't good enough in a city where there is public transportation or an area where a neighbor might give you a ride.

Much time was spent in the early grades disseminating this information so I feel confident in passing it on.

Recognize that what I have just passed on are the

minimum requirements. Venial sins can be committed by not paying proper attention—say letting your mind wander to an activity slated for later that day—or by messing up with the ribbons in the missal. But if you hit at least the minimum you'll get the full point.

In about the fifth grade, all boys were tested for their willingness and ability to accept the responsibility of being altar boys (or alcolytes, the proper term). The nuns advised us that it was an honor to serve as an acolyte and that it was further an honor because no females—nun or otherwise—could ever be an acolyte. Back then, females couldn't enter the sacristy—even while chasing a kid who'd been talking in the lavatory. The sacristy is the area around the altar including places used by the priests and altar boys for Mass preparations. Had we (the young males of that era) been half as bright as we thought we were, we'd have headed for the sacristy anytime we were in trouble. I'm sure the nuns would have waited us out or perhaps sent for the priest to shag us into the open but it might have provided at least a temporary sanctuary.

At any rate, the boys were expected to be acolytes. The kindly old pastor wasn't a real nut on perfection but I strongly suspect that this situation wasn't universal. Our pastor brought us along slowly. If we didn't know the moves or the responses he either whispered the instructions or handled it himself.

Being an altar boy meant serving at daily Mass for a week at a time and then a frequent Sunday assignment. Occasionally there would be a wedding Mass or a funeral Mass. It was common to receive a small stipend, perhaps a quarter or fifty cents, for a wedding or funeral Mass. The pastor typically gave each of the two altar boys a half dollar for serving a week's worth of daily Masses.

Daily Mass was also said for the nuns. I don't believe there was an altar boy at all Masses at the convent but for the infrequent privilege to serve there we were all thankful. You see, after the Mass at the convent, the altar boys were treated to a full breakfast, the same as the nuns would get. The breakfast was fit for a king. After our finishing-up duties, the altar boys (as they emerged from the sacristy) would be greeted by a nun who would usher us down a quiet hall and into a private dining room. I suspect it was a rule that any males in the building would be shielded from the view of the nuns and vice versa. There—in complete privacy and with everything done for us—we ate breakfast. When we were finished we were ushered to the exit. I never felt completely at ease in the convent because males of any age were infrequent guests. Indeed, visitors were rare in the convent. It was the sanctuary of the nuns. it was a unique experience for us as altar boys. We never saw much, though. The only person you ever saw was the nun who served you. The halls in the convent were long and fairly dark and all doors were kept closed. It seemed that the nuns had to stay invisible in their own house.

Being an altar boy involved few hazards. Not knowing the response was a correctable deficiency. Our priest barely took a breath between sentences so our responses as altar boys were hardly missed if we didn't get them in on time. It was about this time that I concluded that everyone in the audience including the altar boys got a full point even if all the responses didn't get in. If this isn't true, there are a lot of disappointed people in hell now.

Can you imagine St. Peter greeting new arrivals at the upstairs office with the message that they hadn't gotten a full point for the Masses at which the altar boys didn't get in the responses? Obviously, lacking the necessary points, they would be carted off to the warmer climate.

During the era in which I was an altar boy, the priest had his back to the congregation when he was saying Mass. The altar boys knelt with their backs to the congregation except when performing a duty. At this point in time there were a large number of duties performed just to add to the pomp and pageantry. One of these duties was the movement of the book, a huge tome from which the priest read the prayers of the Mass. Indeed, the large tome was much like a missal which was commonly used by every member of the congregation. Funny thing though, no matter what the edition of either the missals being used or the priest's Mass book, the version in the priest's book always varied by a few words from the missals used by the congregation. I figured this was because the church hierarchy didn't want anybody to think they had everything down pat. Just when you figured your missal was absolutely perfect the priest rattled off a little different version of the Gospel than you had. That would give you humility again in a hurry.

Anyway, the priest read from the Mass book. For certain parts of the Mass, the book would be to the left side of the altar and the priest would hold his arms out from his body, sort of in an imploring mode, as he read. Later the Mass book would be moved to the other side of the altar and the priest would turn slightly toward that side of the altar and continue reading this time with his arms in front of him. Functionally, the placement of the book didn't seem to matter in my opinion. But it was required that the book be in the right place at the right time. And this duty fell to the acolytes. At the appropriate time, the acolytes would rise from their kneeling positions near the outer edge of the altar, move to the center and genuflect. The "book" boy would then go up the stairs to the book, retrieve it and come to the center beside the waiting acolyte, the two would genuflect in unison and the "book" boy would take the book to the other side of the altar. The person who moved the book made something like a "V" shaped itinerary with the huge tome which obscured his vision of the stairs. Again, there were a few hazards, one of which was negotiating the stairs and missing the bell which was placed strategically in front of the "bell" boy so it would be available to ring at the appropriate times.

On one embarrassing occasion I remember the "book" boy was returning to the center of the altar when he strayed slightly from the required path (or else the bell was slightly out of its proper place) and the "book" boy caught the bell with his foot while in full stride. It skittered crazily and clattered sacreligiously on a path toward the congregation. I saved the day by diving down the stairs and scooping it up with one hand while lying on my belly—much like a major league shortstop might block a hot "grounder."

We—the altar boys—were horribly embarrassed but since the incident occurred before it was permissible to laugh in church no one in the congregation made a sound. Fortunately, it was a Sunday Mass. Had it been a weekday and this had happened in the presence of the nuns this would be a posthumous story.

Chicken And Hamburger On Friday

It was widely disseminated by the nuns that the highest percentage of people in hell were there for obscene (that is, impure) thoughts but the second highest percentage was that of those who had eaten meat on Friday. Few people missed Mass on Sunday back then so this was perhaps fifth or sixth on the list of causes. Being seen in a public place eating meat on Friday would be cause for great scandal (and giving scandal is a mortal sin in itself so you can see that sins increase almost exponentially) and if that meal of meat were financed from church funds the effect of your sins would be roughly equal to that of an adulterous pope.

That leaves me in pretty bad stead on the surface of it. However, I'm relying on the "ignorance" provision. I was ignorant of that fact that it was Friday when I spent money the priest had given me on a 7:30 a.m. hamburger. I might be in trouble on the scandal section though, because I don't think ignorance even protects you in that area.

It was common for the priest to give each of the two altar boys a half dollar at the conclusion of the Friday morning Mass. The boys had served a week's worth of early morning Masses which meant getting up an hour or so earlier than usual and finding a way other than the school bus (usually a ride from a parent) to the church. So it was a little bit of a stipend for the extra service to the church.

On one particular Friday my serving partner and I, upon receiving our half dollars, decided that we had sufficient time to walk to a nearby cafe for breakfast before school started. We probably gave the crusty old waitress a little chuckle when, after considerable deliberation, we selected a chicken salad sandwich (my partner) and a hamburger (for me). It wasn't that she even knew or cared about not eating meat on Friday but she wasn't at all used to seeing people of class and sophistication having chicken salad sandwiches and hamburgers for breakfast.

When we got back to school—ignorant of our blunder—my partner's younger sister inquired about things and we told her of our trip for breakfast. She was aghast that we ate meat on Friday and nearly fainted. Seeing a member of one's family being lost for eternity is not easy to take. But she couldn't contain her newly acquired knowledge and soon was telling everyone in the schoolyard. Certainly, word reached the priest and the nuns. There was nothing the nuns could do for us except maybe arrange for a private confession for us. MORTAL SIN, that was all that raced through anybody's mind. It was the first time the whole world had been aware of one of my serious transgressions.

The seriousness of the mortal sin was probably compounded by the use of money from a priest. Speaking only for myself, I've learned to live with the igominy. I just hope that we, the altar boys, didn't take the kindly old priest down with us.

chapter six

Sex was a word not used in class so it was usually expressed as "boy-girl relationships." What we knew for sure was that God didn't want any messing around and associating with persons of the other sex (we only knew of heterosexual tendencies) was a potential occasion of sin which we were all duty bound to avoid. Occasions of sin can occur anywhere and they are different for everyone but there are apparently a lot of them that are common to everybody. For instance, a person with a weakness for drink might find all bars and liquor stores occasions of sin and, therefore, would be duty-bound to avoid them. He would be obligated to plan his paths to and from work so as not to pass any such establishments. As another example, women with a tendency to gossip might be duty-bound to avoid coffee klatches as occasions of sin. I think this one might be quite rare.

A young male with a tendency to day dream and occasionally harbor an obscene (aka impure) thought might be duty bound to avoid waking hours. He would have to sleep at all times when he wasn't occupying his mind with academic matters. Because impure thoughts can occur even in church, this is a particularly difficult one to handle. Better consult your confessor here.

Enough of teaching, however, and back to the original topic, contact between boys and girls between the ages of 11 and 33. According to the official teaching of the nuns, there wasn't to be any contact except in academic matters and they should be kept to a minimum. But the damnable practice of boy meeting girl persisted and continues to persist even to this very day. And, I suspect, if the nuns couldn't stamp it out, it's a tough evil to eradicate.

Boy-girl parties were something the nuns handled poorly. Everybody knew that they were expressly forbidden in the Old and New Testaments, the Baltimore Catechism and everywhere else. Indeed, this proscription might be the closest thing to the eleventh commandment that I know of.

Still—and I mean still—in the face of all the evidence of the evil nature of boy-girl parties in about the sixth grade they would start taking place. It was generally thought back then that it was the parents of the girls who were most lax in the area of preventing these.

So it became the obligation of the nuns to ferret out the sources of evil. How the nuns ever found out I don't know but I suppose there were snitches even back then. Anyway, on Monday mornings (since most boy-girl parties took place on the weekends) the nuns would commence what I termed "witch hunts." One girl at a time would be called out of the room and, I believe, questioned in the principal's office. Often, the nun and the girl would be crying when they re-entered the room. This wasn't an easy task for anyone. Usually, then, a second girl would be called from the room. The way I interpreted it, the snitch probably just knew the name of someone who had been at or hosted a boy-girl party over the weekend. So that suspected hostess or attendee would be the first called from the room.

But, I suppose, the snitch's information was rarely correct or complete so many people (usually girls) would have to be questioned to get the correct site of the party and complete guest list.

It was good to be male then because males were generally exempt from the questioning and punishment. I'm sure it was recognized by the nuns that sixth grade and older boys just grow up to be sinful men anyway. To the extent that statistics support this, it isn't a bad generalization. Punishments were meted out to the offending girls, though I don't think you can ever say enough rosaries to make up for a boy-girl party.

However stiff these punishments were—and I assume calls to the parents were included—it was never fully effective. The Monday morning syndrome of witch hunts continued from the sixth through eighth grades after which point boys and girls were separated in school.

Preparations began for Confession in first grade. In recent years it has become known by a popular euphemism—The Sacrament of Reconciliation. But nothing fits quite like Confession. And it was done "right" back in those days—dark box, priest separated by a screen and long lines outside the confessional.

For those who don't remember, a brief description of the set-up is in order. A confessional usually consisted of three adjacent closet-like boxes about three feet by five feet. The confessional was located in a rear corner of the church. Indeed, each church had two or three confessionals. Remember, business in this area was much better then. Most people went to confession at least once a month and often weekly. The center box of each confessional held the priest who sat in a chair facing outward. The front of the priest's box usually had a standard looking door or maybe a half-door. The lower half would be a wooden door and the upper half a heavy, dark drapery-material curtain. The boxes on each side of the priest were used by the confessing persons. A sliding door a foot or so square connected the confessing person's box with the priest. A solid door-like cover was opened and closed over a screen-like material. With the wood door in an open position, sound would pass between priest and person confessing but only shapes were visible. The priest's box was just light enough so you could see his form sitting in a chair. Usually he'd have his ear almost against the opening. That was so you didn't have to whisper very loudly.

The confessional box was quite dark so at best the priest could see a human form. Indeed, he could see just the head of the person whose confession he was hearing. This, of course, was planned. The priest wasn't supposed to know whose confession he was hearing.

There would be a person in each confessional box and the priest would hear the confession of one with the door to the opposite opening closed. Upon completion of that confession he'd close the door to that box and open the other. While the changeover of persons was taking place on one side he'd be hearing a confession from the other side. It was a good system. There was some efficiency there and pretty good security.

While we're on the subject of security, it is appropriate to point out that there was a system of lights to tell waiting persons which confessionals were occupied. The confessing person knelt on a kneeler (thus, confessing his sins in a kneeling position to the sitting priest) facing the opening to the priest's box. The kneeler was spring loaded so that a switch would be off when no one was kneeling on it. As you hit a kneeling position, your weight would depress the kneeler a fraction of an inch (making the switch) so that a small bulb would light outside the confessional. That would notify those in line that the confessional was occupied. Obviously, this was a worry to newcomers to confession. The worry: "what if someone comes in here while I'm rattling off my sins?" has caused everyone from Adam onward to sweat. It was, however, not a genuine cause for concern. In all my time in and around confessionals, I never saw anybody but a nun go into an occupied confessional. And, in this case, the nun was on a mission of mercy. She went in to notify a young penitent that he was whispering in a loud voice.

This description of confessionals might not be entirely universal but I don't think they varied much.

It was dark in the priest's box and in the confession sections. I don't know for sure what the purpose of darkness was but the situation made it frightening to newcomers. Priest and confessing person whispered. This was merely to prevent people from overhearing. Once in a while a very young person or a hard-of-hearing person might raise his or her voice a little too much but this was very rare.

The object of confession was to tell the priest your sins so that he could forgive them. You can't forgive if you don't know what you're being asked to forgive was the reason given for the requirement of listing your sins. God knew but the priest didn't. It was pointed out by the nuns and priests that only mortal—that is, the serious—sins really had to be confessed. The venial (less serious) sins, if omitted by accident of memory or otherwise, would still be forgiven. On the other hand, a mortal sin omitted would not be forgiven and the conscious omission of such a sin only compounded matters because now you had a "bad" confession on your hands, too. A "bad" confession was also a mortal sin so you can see again how sins can be thought to increase exponentially.

When the process of training for confession was initiated in the first grade, a whole lot of people involved were short on mortal sins so a list of venial sins was all that you could come up with. You must remember that one couldn't sin until reaching the age of reason which is about seven years of age so most first graders were lucky to have committed their first hundred or so sins before their first confessions.

Fortunately, as time went on, we could come up with a list of reasonable length without a lot of trouble. You see, the time in the confessional was a sign to the outside world. If it was too short, then you must be a goody-goody who never did anything wrong. There were few of us who had this problem.

Now, one might live through this type of ignominy because memories in regard to this side of the spectrum are very short. But try telling a first- or second-grader that. At that point in time a half-day seems like an eternity. In

"I'D EVEN TAKE A BILLION 'HAIL MARYS' AS A PENANCE."

fact, to first graders the nuns explained the concept of eternity by saying that it was longer than it took to get from first grade to eighth grade. That scared the hell out of most people.

The other side of the coin was worse. If you were in the confessional a long time, everybody knew you did something exotic. Nobody ever considered that it might be just a large number of routine sins that kept you in there, or that you talked slowly, or that the priest had a funny story to tell.

I'm here to say that it wasn't always the fault of the person confessing that it took a long time. He or she might very well have had a pretty moderate list of routine stuff but he'd hit the priest's hot button with a thousand impure thoughts or something and you'd be in for a tongue lashing that might last several minutes. I used to pray that no matter what the priest had to say that he would say it fast. I'd even take a billion Hail Marys as a penance if he'd get it over with fast. To this day, my personal record is a half-billion Hail Marys and a million Our Fathers and I think I got this on the priest's bad day.

A penance could be a minor problem, too, because immediately after confession each person returned to a pew in the church to say his or her penance. Again, if it were a modest penance, one might be able to satisfy it quickly thus not revealing the serious nature of your sins. What protected a vast number of people was that it was not mandatory that the entire penance be done right after confession. So those of religious savvy would do a modest amount of their penance in the pew, make the sign of the cross (as though completed) and get up and leave only to complete the penance in private later. I'm sure this was frowned on by the nuns. But I'm also sure it was no more than a venial sin.

Confession was mandatory on an annual basis. But, at the grade school level, it was encouraged on a weekly basis. The encouragement usually took the form of holding confession during school hours and sending each person. In other words, mandatory weekly confession.

Preparation for confession culminated with first confession near the end of first grade. First confession was celebrated but not with quite the same pomp and pageantry as first communion would be a year or so later. Now, some seeding had to be done for the first confession. It is not unfair to say that some of us were so dumb we didn't even know what we'd done wrong. But the nun assured us that we'd all sinned.

An examination of conscience was to be made by going through the Ten Commandments and various Church laws. While we did this in the classroom, we didn't, of course, have to let anyone see what we were writing. Indeed, we just made a mental list. At the age of six or seven, the Ten Commandments were very frightening. Most of us preparing for first confession really didn't have to worry a lot about violating many of the commandments, though. We were quickly advised by the teaching nun that we'd have to wait a while before worrying about commiting adultery or coveting thy neighbor's wife. What she didn't tell us was how long and it seemed like forever to me.

Coveting thy neighbor's bicycle might be a concern or missing Mass on Sunday. But this was rare because for almost everyone the entire family went to Mass at once so there was about as much chance of missing Mass as there was of commiting adultery.

So the nun typically had to seed the usual—lying, tardiness to school, disobeying parents, fighting with brothers and sisters and, the most serious, disobeying the nun. Most of the nuns wanted disobeying a nun to be raised to the status of a mortal sin but there was no effective lobbying force then. Chronic and persistent disobedience of the teaching nun could eventually reach the status of a mortal sin but I think this loophole was rarely used by the nuns.

Numbers could be a problem. Obviously, with each confession of a sin, the number of times one had committed it was required information. Usually, one could take a good guess and setting the number became less of a problem as time went on because each person sort of settled in on his own numbers. They would be reasonable numbers that you were comfortable with and that the priest wouldn't get too excited about. If you thought he might remember the number of impure thoughts from your last confession, you could increment the number downward slightly without seriously abridging fact. "Good numbers" were numbers that more or less fit on a long-term basis. I didn't know it at the time but this was my first training in statistics. Today I am more scrupulous and include with the Mean (or Average) a Standard Deviation so the priest has a better idea of the normal curve under which I am operating.

So a typical early confession or first confession might be: since my last confession two weeks ago I've lied about 10 times (the word "about" is a significant hedge against committing a venial sin of slightly altering the exact number), disobeyed about 12 times, fought with my brother three times, was tardy to school once and threw rocks at a dog once. Of course as the years went by this list changed mostly to include impure thoughts and a few boy-girl parties.

First confession at a slightly older age—third or fourth grade—was tried a few years ago but was soon officially discouraged by the Church. Confession at a very early age ingrains a certain guilt that is good to have. Otherwise you can get out of the habit of confession.

The study of sins was very important because, obviously, one had to know the sins themselves and the category (venial or mortal) in order to make a good confession. So, as preparation for first confession, much time was spent on sins. As the years went by even more time was spent on the study of sins. And we were advised by the nuns that priests spent vastly more time studying sins so that they would be sure to know all the sins. That way they would never be ignorant of what the confessing person was talking about. And, it was emphasized, that because of this vast expertise in the area of sin, we never needed to worry about shocking a priest. This is, indeed, true. But I swear I've heard a whooshing of air from the priest's lungs similar to what might happen when a person is truly surprised. Yet I've never heard a priest say, "Sonofagun, I never heard of that one." On occasions, I thought I've heard a rippling of pages, perhaps indicitive of the priest the looking through a huge tome for a certain sin.

It is genuinely too bad that the Church changed confession to eliminate the listing of sins. It has eliminated a rich source of Catholic jokes. Have you heard the one about the priest who had a date to golf with a buddy after confession on Saturday afternoon? Usually the buddy is described as a rabbi. It seems that the lines of those waiting to confess were unusually long that afternoon. So the priest hearing confessions and the rabbi, waiting not so patiently in the vestibule, grew more and more concerned that it would get too late to go golfing if something wasn't done to speed things up.

So the priest said to the rabbi: "You listen to one of my confessions to get the hang of it and then you take the other confessional. Nobody will ever know the difference." So the rabbi slipped in with the priest and the first person to come in was a woman who confessed to committing adultery three times. The priest told the woman to say 10 Hail Marys, 10 Our Fathers and to put $30 in the Sunday collection and her sins would then be forgiven. Obviously, this happened before inflation hit so hard.

With this minimal training the rabbi took over in another confessional. As luck would have it, his first penitent was a woman who confessed to committing adultery once. To which the rabbi responded: "Say 10 Hail Marys, 10 Our Fathers, put $30 in the collection tomorrow and you've got twice more coming."

See what we've lost?

In a more serious vein, it was mandatory to categorize sins. Venial were the little things like lying and disobeying if done moderately and on a small scale. Tardiness to school was typically thought of as venial. Stealing could go mortal or venial depending on the amount involved.

Back then a dollar was a good break-off point. Under was a venial sin, over was mortal. But as time went on and inflation edged things upward at the rate of three to four percent a year, this figure had to be tied to inflation. (And you thought COLAs were new.) The break-off became a day's pay of the wronged party. That is, if you stole the equivalent of less than a day's pay from someone it was probably a venial sin. Greater than a day's pay was undoubtedly a mortal sin. I've heard nothing in recent years to indicate that this rule of thumb is no longer valid. Obviously, it has its weaknesses, however. Anyone with an ounce of brains would steal only from the highly compensated. To steal from an unemployed person is folly.

The obvious mortal sins—murder, missing Mass on Sunday or a Holy Day of Obligation and impure thoughts—needed no definition or break-off points. Theological discussions could be developed in the areas of whether or not giving less than the appropriate percentage of your income to the church was a mortal or venial sin. Not sending your children to a Catholic school was a mortal sin. In the first few grades those matters didn't trouble us but we needed the knowledge for future years.

Of course, most sins could be aligned with a commandment, which made them convenient to memorize. Because it wasn't always obvious which commandment was being violated, there is a category of random sins. An example would be entering a non-Catholic church without good cause. Good, valid reasons for placing one's body in a non-Catholic church might be a very close friend's wedding or funeral. Other religious celebrations were not good or valid reasons. And the friend (or perhaps relative) had to be a life-long non-Catholic and come from a history of non-Catholic tradition. In other words, only someone who could possibly be free of the mortal sin of rejecting Catholic teaching. That's why I was so careful in the area of relatives. Relatives could be assumed to have been exposed to Catholic teaching and must have rejected it or they wouldn't still be non-Catholics. So attending a wedding or funeral of a non-Catholic relative was treading on dangerous ground. In recent years, this directive has been relaxed or else it is being widely ignored.

The actual participation in the non-Catholic service was to be minimized. No action on the part of the Catholic was permitted. Action on the part of the Catholic which might be construed as participation in the service was absolutely forbidden (under pain of a double mortal sin, I assume). That's why Catholics never participated in non-Catholic weddings or funerals. You just couldn't be too safe.

While attending a non-Catholic service one was forbidden to do anything more than sit. Standing, singing, or throwing a buck in the collection basket was a certain trip downstairs.

Preparation For First Communion

Preparation for first communion took place basically in the second grade, the year after first confession. There was a certain amount of understanding required and everyone had to have time to obtain the required wearing apparel. All girls wore little white dresses and patent leather shoes. Boys had to have dress pants, a white shirt, tie and leather shoes. Then the kids were arranged from shortest to tallest so the procession into the church would look good. The kids assembled in their class rooms just before Mass time. Usually this would be an early morning Mass sometime in early May. On cue, they proceeded into the church two abreast, shortest to tallest. As each pair reached the appropriate pew, the pair genuflected together and went into the pew. First communicants sat in the forward pews, boys and girls on opposite sides of the center aisle, with their relatives behind them. All the kids in the second grade made their first communion at the same time. In our parish that was perhaps 100 kids from the school and a handful of kids who attended public school. The public school kids would receive special training outside of their regular school time so they could take part in the first communion activities. The first communion preparation was one of the few times Catholic kids who didn't go to the Catholic school were brought together with the Catholic school kids. If our parish was representative, fewer than 10 percent of Catholic kids went to public grade schools.

Family involvement in the ceremony itself was minimal. Not like today when it's more of a family affair. The parents then didn't participate in the planning or execution. That was the domain of the nuns. The nuns liked to have a special tribute to the Virgin Mary so one or two select girls would go to the statue of the Virgin Mary with a bouquet of flowers.

Afterward all assembled outside the church for pictures and conversation with family and friends. Nuns breathed a huge collective sigh of relief when it was all over and there were no great goofs. Funny, though, the nuns disappeared after the Mass. They didn't circulate widely among the families. It was still forbidden for them to spend time with lay people. It must have been that lay people were a potential source of temptation. Nuns really seemed to like kids and families even though it was entirely outside the requirements of being a nun that a nun might show any affection for a kid or lay person.

For first communion one had to learn the precepts of the Eucharist (including how to stick out your tongue properly) and the requirements of the communion fast.

The communion fast commenced at midnight the night before you were to receive communion and it proscribed food or water. Again, as in many areas there were some exceptions. You might be allowed to take doctor-prescribed medications and maybe even some water to wash down a pill but only if the doctor expressly advised that the medication be taken with water. It was advisable to avoid this situation as much as possible because, if one were to abuse this privilege by taking more than the minimum amount of water, it could be construed as breaking the fast.

Brushing of teeth was particularly precarious because, while it was permissible to rinse one's mouth with water, it was not permissible to swallow any. More than one kid spent time agonizing over the predicatment of having made an involuntary swallow. You couldn't be sure that you hadn't swallowed water so the safest interpretation was to assume that you had broken the fast and not receive communion that day. But that situation almost certainly meant explaining to brothers, sisters and parents, who would scowl fiercely at your stupidity. That is, if they believed you at all.

It seems paradoxical in retrospect, considering that it

was so easy to break the communion fast, that not going to communion was generally taken to mean that one was not in the State of Grace. So the fool who accidentally broke his or her communion fast would almost certainly get misjudged. The elders would glower at you as they went to communion. You'd be there in a seated position while those going to communion would be obliged to squeeze past you to get to the aisle. And the younger kids would give you a knowing look (another impure thought had gotten you). I'm sure many people had the temptation to form their hand as though around a water glass and make a motion toward the mouth as though drinking water so as to give an indication to those around that they'd really just broken the fast and weren't necessarily in a state of serious sin. I never saw anybody do that but I did see people whose mouths were moving as the people squeezed by them. I assumed they were telling their side of the story, such as "I woke up out of a sound sleep and took a small drink of water before I even knew what I was doing." I'd never have tried that. It's too dumb to believe.

Obviously, the thoughtless taking of a drink of water was the greatest threat to accidentally breaking the communion fast. It was just understood that no one would purposely break the fast. So, at our house, water faucets were covered by towels on Saturday night before bedtime. That way, even in a state of drowsiness, the presence of a towel over the faucet should jerk you into alertness before you got any water in you.

You can tell a good Catholic by the way he or she sticks out his or her tongue. A good crisp thrust outward coupled with a straight, horizontal lay is the product of good training and considerable experience at it. I've heard that other religions use this technique so don't use this as a

"ANOTHER IMPURE THOUGHT HAD GOTTEN YOU."

discerning test for Catholics.

The reason for this is that until very recently everybody received communion on his or her tongue. One of my most frequent prayers as a youth was that all priests meticulously washed their hands just before Mass. It was horribly frequent occurrence to get a thumb print from the priest laying the host on your tongue. Yuck.

Now when receiving of communion was done right (I say that tongue in cheek—I just couldn't resist), people knelt at a communion rail and the priest proceeded from his left to right to distribute communion. The altar boy's function during communion time was more meaningful then. He moved with the priest and held the platen under the chin of each person as he or she received communion. After the person received, he or she stood up and returned to his place in the pew and another took his place at the communion rail. It was really quite an orderly process but it was more time-consuming than the present practice of receiving in a standing position.

In the fifties, perhaps half of the attendees at Mass received communion. Now it's closer to 90 percent. In the "old" days you had the kids who were too young to receive, those who messed up on their communion fast and those not in the State of Grace. I believe the number not in the State of Grace was vastly exaggerated because there were a lot of scrupulous people who worried excessively about their sins. But, because of the lower percentage of people receiving communion, a Sunday Mass could be finished in 35 minutes.

Had the communion rail not gone the way of the altar that faced the wall, I hate to think how long a Sunday

Mass might take nowadays with 90-some percent of the people going to communion.

Lent, that 40-day period from Ash Wednesday through Holy Saturday (the day before Easter), was always a difficult period, as it was intended to be. But the spirit of penance is an unusual one for kids six through 13 years of age (the grade school years). At that point in your life you sort of look for loopholes. For instance, it was virtually mandatory that you "give up" something for lent. Now that was no small sacrifice because lent was 40 days and 40 nights—as everyone knew. The only thing that could mitigate the lenten sacrifice was that under a liberal interpretation Sundays could be excluded. So whatever sacrifice you made for lent might still be indulged in on Sundays. However, it was sort of subliminally implanted by the nuns that this was the easy way out and it was spiritually better for you not to take advantage of that loophole.

What you gave up for lent could be missed for a long time. Nothing was longer than lent. Now the 'ster would interrogate each pupil in the days immediately preceeding Ash Wednesday as to what he/she was going to "give up." Nothing was not an option. So you prepared by mentally going down the list of usuals—candy, gum and movies. Movies, first, were almost expected. There was to be no special entertainment during lent so movies were out anyway. If you chose to take the risk of indicating to 'ster that you were giving up movies, you'd better be prepared to add to the list.

If you chose to tell the nun that you were giving up gum you took a risk, as well. Nuns weren't dumb. They weren't born yesterday. They knew that people who never chewed gum might be inclined to "give up" gum for lent. So, if you said you were giving up gum, you'd better be ready to swear that you were a two-pack-a-day person at least.

All that really left was candy. Everybody liked candy so if you told 'ster you were giving up candy for lent, you'd usually get an acknowledging smile.

Usually, all forms of entertainment were suspended for lent. The school and church would sponsor no activities. Mother-daughter breakfasts, father-son breakfasts and so forth were suspended. It always seemed like a Protestant conspiracy to me that the Shrine circus showed up in town during lent. So the circus was out unless a Protestant friend could sneak you a ticket.

chapter seven

Mention of pagan babies isn't unique to this story of a Catholic education but a chronicle of Catholic education would not be complete without a discussion of pagan babies. The practice of ransoming pagan babies must have been universal in Catholic grade schools. In our school, pagan babies cost $5 and it usually took some time to collect that much because it came from kids in nickel and dime amounts. To speed things up and increase the number of pagan babies ransomed, the nun often pitted the boys against the girls. It would be a race to see which could get enough money first. The nun might ask everyone to give up candy or gum for a week and put the money saved into the pagan baby fund. A canister would be provided for the boys and another for the girls and the amount each had collected would be posted conspicuously. The frenzy of the competition enveloped everybody. As time went on (inflation, of course), it became easier to collect $5, so we merely purchased more pagan babies. There was, to my knowledge, no quantity discount.

When the amount reached the desired objective, the

nun sent the money off to whomever handled the actual purchases. We never heard from any of the pagan babies, so I don't know what became of them. But there certainly must be millions of them who were purchased over the years. I can only guess that the supply was unlimited because the price never went up and no one ever had to order ahead.

It isn't in fashion to discuss this nowadays, but back then we readily accepted the information that there were a lot of people in foreign lands who needed the Catholic religion. If we didn't get there first, the area might fall into the hands of the Protestants. The missionaries and nuns would tell us of vast areas heavily populated by pagans which were left untouched. They'd also tell us of previous successes. For example, the missionary who arrived in an area to find the people eating each other and worshiping idols. Within a week he'd have them converted, a church built, and a knee-high corn crop. Shortly to follow would be the school. When it was necessary, I assume that driving out the Protestant missionaries was done discreetly.

India was big. We all knew them as the starving people of India. South America was occasionally brought up but this was thought to be secure area because the vast majority of people were already Catholic. Perhaps some attending to their physical needs was in order but otherwise they were all right.

Catholic grade schools didn't have the latest and best of everything—maybe anything. So making do was a way of life. At our school, gymnasium facilities were really on the "Rube Goldberg" end of the spectrum. In a room that tripled as a lunchroom, gymnasium and meeting room (outside of school hours), we had a basketball court you'd hardly believe. While the room was long enough and wide enough to provide a semblance of a basketball game, it was far less than 10-feet high. So the baskets were affixed such that the backboards were butted against the ceiling. That left the rim of the basket a couple of feet short of the regulation 10-foot height. But worse than that, the low overhead prevented any arc to the shot. Wilt Chamberlain would have hit his head on the ceiling dunking the ball.

While dunking the ball wasn't a factor in a game involving five-foot grade schoolers, a little arc is almost a necessity for a shot from say seven or eight feet out (the long ones). Most of the time a shot of that length hit the ceiling and caromed back to the floor. A hard shot could kill or maim a player too slow to get away from the ball on its return trip from the ceiling. An arching pass from a point-guard being looped in to a 5-7 center might hit the ceiling, too. If memory serves me correctly, the ball was dead upon hitting the ceiling so it meant a lot of jump-balls and throw-ins.

The facilities, while conducive to developing good dribblers and line-drive shooters, were not conducive to high-scoring games so contests of 2-0 and 4-2 were relatively common. To my knowledge, no one from our grade school ever went on to play professional basketball.

Though the overwhelming majority of teachers in Catholic grade schools were nuns, there were a few lay teachers. Even the name—lay teachers—sounds funny nowadays. Lay teachers were—and are—non-Religious teachers. Not really "non-religious" just not members of a religious order. In simple terms that means non-nuns.

In the time I'm talking about, grade school lay teachers were always women, always married, usually had kids in the school and usually had most of the same attributes as nuns. That is, they had to be fervent, pious and willing to work for low pay. They had to accept that chewing gum in school was a mortal sin and that talking in the lavatory broke a commandment (which one I don't remember).

Only one or two lay teachers were allowed per school. I assume this was because of the relative abundance of nuns as opposed to the relative scarcity today. Lay teachers did about the same things as nuns except, as I remember, they didn't teach religion. In years when the grade was taught by a lay teacher we had a nun or a priest teach the religion class. Typically, lay teachers didn't hit kids as much. Some were just as strict as nuns but others were less so. I think it was because they had kids of their own and knew what it was like to treat bruises outside of school hours. If I remember correctly, the lay teachers with kids past grade school age tended to have more of the stricter attributes while the lay teachers with kids of grade-school age tended to have more understanding tendencies and meted out less pain and misery.

The issue of lay teachers seems to be one place where Catholic dogma left a loophole. I don't remember hearing how many lay teachers a kid could have through grade school years and still go to heaven. You'll have to invoke some "Hope" here. I'd say if the number is one or two you ought to be safe.

Catholic school kids loved Holy Days. Those were the days when public school kids had to go to school and Catholic school kids didn't. Public school kids hated Holy Days, out of jealousy, I'm sure.

Five of the six Holy Days practiced by the Catholic Church fell during the school year. Unfortunately, two of them, Christmas and the Feast of the Circumcision, which was New Year's Day, fell during a period when we weren't in school (Christmas vacation). That left two in the fall (November 1 and December 8) and one in the spring (Ascension Thursday, 40 days after Easter) as non-school days. Oh, how we felt cheated when November 1 or December 8 fell on a Saturday or Sunday.

It was obligatory under pain of mortal sin to attend Mass on Holy Days. But, after that, you, as a Catholic school kid, were free. Just like a Sunday, you might say. To the Catholic school kids, Holy Days were thought to be over-rated. The public school kids were green with envy, but the Holy Days really weren't that good. The public school kids were tied up, so games that took a large number of kids were out. There wasn't TV and radio was dull in the daytime. So the Catholic school kids just waited around for the end of the school day anyway when they could resume normal activities with public school kids.

Public school administrators and Catholic school administrators didn't like Holy Days. Because a low percentage of Catholic school kids tended to show up at the public schools just to do a little disrupting, the public school administrators would call the Catholic school administrators to complain. The next day there would be an inquest. Catholic school administrators (nuns) being more successful than the FBI, the violators were generally identified. Still, there remained a hositlity between administrators. The Catholic school administrators tended to think that their counterparts in the public schools over-rated the problem. And, I suppose, it was hard for the

"NO ONE FROM OUR GRADE SCHOOL EVER WENT ON TO PLAY
PROFESSIONAL BASKETBALL."

nuns to completely suppress the thought that, if the public school kids and administrators were alert to the missionary work around them, the whole world would be Catholic and we wouldn't need public schools.

Hot Lunches

Lacking the financial resources of public schools, which had a full hot lunch program, Catholic grade schools sometimes had scaled-down versions. Ours had a policy of a hot entree (soup or chili) or something else such as jello. Fridays, meatless days, were usually the days we had jello. The school also served milk and, like the public schools, the milk price was subsidized so a half-pint carton of milk was two or three cents.

One person could—and did—handle the kitchen duties from preparing to cleaning up. Mothers of the kids were expected to donate a certain number of lunch hours a year to help clean up after lunch.

Kids brought their basic lunch from home in a brown bag or metal lunch box. Lunch boxes were socially acceptable when you were in the low grades but as you got older lunch boxes went out. Carrying a lunch box just wasn't in vogue then. To supplement the sandwiches, cookies or cake from home, a kid purchased the entree of the day and milk.

The "chili" days were especially favored. The kids who really liked chili—and I was among them—would go back two or three times. You had to pay each time but it was well worth it. The jello was favored too.

Waste was always a bugaboo with the nuns. We got a new principal about the seventh grade who was really a nut on waste. It was observed by the nuns that certain kids regularly threw away part of their lunch. Maybe an uneaten portion of a sandwich or worse yet a whole sandwich. Some mothers just seemed to pack too big a lunch or include certain undesirable items.

Waste was particularly abhorrent because of the starving children of India. We didn't know it at the time but there were starving people a lot closer than India.

So the principal (they taught us to spell principle and principal by noting that in reference to the school administrator the word ended in "pal" so I, therefore, thought a pal was somebody who smiled just before she hit you) made a rule that no one would leave the lunchroom with any of his or her lunch uneaten. The principal stationed herself near the door to the lunchroom and each exiting pupil was obliged to show evidence that there was no uneaten food concealed in wrappings he or she was tossing out.

But this system didn't work for long. Some kids whose mothers packed unreasonably large lunches were in danger of spending the rest of their years in the lunchroom. Sure, some of the kids ate things they ordinarily wouldn't have. But that wasn't always good. And there was a certain amount of trading of food. Dessert items could be traded or given away, as I recall, but half-eaten sandwiches were a bear to get rid of.

Some of us were obliged to eat cellophane wrapping and all when a package wouldn't open. The older kids probably handled the situation better than the younger ones who panicked when they couldn't get their milk carton open. We'd just gone from milk bottles to paper milk cartons about that time.

Some kids turned to trickery—a risk few prudent people took because, Lord knows, the penalty for the original violation was severe (including the automatic mortal sin). But the penalty for compounding the violation by concealment of uneaten food was undoubtedly a capital crime. Some kids stuffed half-eaten sandwiches in their pockets while others slipped half-eaten things in the lunch bag of the kid next to him. And one thing the exit-monitoring principal wouldn't "buy" was the contention that the half-eaten food in your lunch bag was put there by someone else. The "pal" wasn't born yesterday.

It must have been greasy pants pockets and large numbers of kids who were unable to pass the exit inspection that caused the nun to change the system. It became acceptable for a kid who couldn't eat an item from his lunch to put it on one of several large trays put near the exit for this purpose. Uneaten (but not half-eaten) items could be left on a tray so that one could pass the exit inspection either by eating all of his or her lunch or by having put unwanted articles on the tray. What was left on the trays, obviously, was suitable for human consumption and therefore was not, per se, being wasted. Indeed, kids might add to their lunch with items from the trays which tended to gather an assortment of sandwiches, pieces of cake, cookies and other things. Most lunch hours ended with two or three trays of uneaten articles.

What the nuns did with this stuff I don't remember. I

doubt that they shipped it to the starving kids in India considering the cost and fact that most of it would have been pretty dry by the time it got there.

Nowadays there are large programs to give instruction in Catholicism to Catholic kids who attend public schools. In the old days this was unheard of. There were so few kids who fell in that category that the situation could be safely ignored.

To some extent, Sunday was easier on Catholic school kids than on non-Catholic school kids. The non-Catholic school kids, Catholic or Protestant, often had to attend Sunday school which consumed an hour or more each Sunday morning. Catholic school kids could attend a fast Mass and be free for the day. At our parish we had a 35-minute Mass that drew people from miles around. Sunday school, which, according to the reports I heard, was more fun than regular school, still took more time than Mass.

Anyway, there were always a few Catholic kids who didn't attend the Catholic school. They would get some instruction in a Sunday-school situation and then make the sacraments with the Catholic school kids. Things like CCD (the Catholic program for religious instruction of non-Catholic-school kids) were unheard of.

Converts

There really isn't much to say about converts because there were so few made by Catholic kids that I knew. We were generally failures along this line. Part of our commission as educated Catholic kids was to go out into the Protestant world and make converts. But the only place we could reasonably hope to get them from was among our non-Catholic friends and they were by Catholic mandate limited to few (if any) in number. Just walking down the street making converts was tough even back then.

But the nuns told us: "Go out and make converts. There are a lot of people out there whom God wants. Convert 'em. The priests and nuns are in foreign countries doing the job." We were supposed to do it in the good old U.S.A.

If there is any area in which I feel unusually weak, this is it. As far as I know I've never converted anybody. I'm slightly guilt ridden because I never had the guts to approach someone on the street and try to convert him or her. I guess it is because I'm basically shy and also because I figured anyone who was that aggressive about it had better have the Baltimore Catechism memorized word for word because a potential convert was likely to ask a lot of questions. "Which is the one true church?" is the only question I knew the answer to.

As much as nuns valued converts and worked on us to get them, I think this aspect of our training was the least successful. And I think the nuns might have secretly known this because the area of converts was about the only one not tallied on a chart in the classroom.

The Legion of Decency protected us from the sinful movies. A group of people (I never knew one who sat on the Legion of Decency so I can only go on what I heard second and third hand), mostly priests, I think, viewed every movie that was released and rated each one.

Before a Catholic could attend a movie, he or she must check the Legion of Decency rating to make sure that the movie was acceptable to the Legion of Decency. It was an automatic sin to see a movie with an unacceptable rating. I'm not sure if it was a venial or a mortal sin but almost everybody observed the rule so I suspect it was widely thought to be a mortal sin.

Large groups of teenagers would be in the vestibule of the church on Saturday evening checking the Legion of Decency list. It was several pages long in very small type. (You must remember all movies had to be listed.) All Catholic churches had the Legion of Decency list posted conspicuously.

Movies that could be seen were rated "A." The system I believe was soon revised to an A-1, A-2, A-3 scheme so that slight differentiations could be made. An A-1 for instance was acceptable for all; A-2 might be acceptable for those over 12; and A-3 for adults only. Movies rated "B" or "C" could be seen only by the members of the Legion of Decency. Rumors to the contrary, I'm not convinced that the legion had to view the "C" movies two or three times to make up their minds.

The Legion of Decency ratings sure made life tough for the teenagers. Maybe there'd be two or three theaters within commuting distance and they'd all be showing movies unsuitable for Catholic teenagers.

Now you bring that up at the appropriate time in religion class and the kindly priest would tell you to organize your parents, friends and relatives and write letters to the theater owners telling them that you weren't going to patronize their establishments if they didn't quit showing "bad" movies. I'm sure that scared the hell out of theater owners.

Conversations in the Church vestibule on Saturday evening used to go something like this. A person would elbow his or her way through the group to get close enough to read the Legion of Decency rating. The person would be saying, "hey, what's the rating on "The Speck-led Pup meets Little Orphan Annie?" "B," somebody would holler back. This might seem like a minor point at this time but it's essential to point out that you couldn't go on somebody else's memory or observation. You had to see the rating with your own eyes. Some people tried to fake their way by telling the nun on Monday morning that a friend or another member of the family had said the movie was an "A." If you didn't actually see the list yourself it was just as much a sin as if you never troubled yourself to check at all.

Anyway, the "B" rating would shake up plans fast. "How could it be," the surprised teenager might exclaim. "Mary Jo (a non-Catholic) saw it and said there was nothing bad about it." But the Legion of Decency saw something. Maybe the movie showed the pup going to the bathroom against a tree or maybe the pup panted when he was looking at Little Orphan Annie. Anyway the Legion of Decency had it's way.

A big reason for "B" ratings was "suggestive costum-ing." That meant the ladies didn't have enough on. "Sug-gestive situations" was another. And that meant one of the couples in the movie (married or unmarried) was getting pretty worked up or maybe a teenage couple was shown alone in a house.

Portaying divorce as an acceptable situation was another reason for a "B" rating. If a couple was considering divorce but both members were portrayed as being very anguished about it and got back together again at the end it might escape the bad rating. There couldn't be any fooling around by either during the anguishing period or it was an automatic "B."

Now a "C" meant condemned. That usually meant the ladies didn't have anything on. Or maybe the Church wasn't shown in a favorable light. Perhaps people were shown eating meat on Friday, or maybe not going to confession during Eastertime. Anyway, it was a "C" and nobody could see it.

Well, the movie you were going to see was a "B" so you checked to see what was showing at another theater. Somebody always brought the movie listings from the newspaper. Pretty soon you'd despair. It was getting close to starting time and the only "A" movies were ones you'd seen.

Usually, that meant either seeing a movie a second time or going home to read a book about your favorite saint. (You can believe that last part if you want to.)

NO TALKING IN THE LAVATORY 137.

chapter eight

Geography was a subject that was presented with intense vigor. Since I hadn't seen anything further from home than where my relatives lived 500 miles away, I found geography very interesting. The text books were written so as to be easy to relate to, which I did. As each country was introduced, a kid about our age was made part of the lesson. The kid's life could be compared to ours. Most of the time there was a family of four—mother, father, son and daughter—just like home. I really think that if the texts were written by good Catholic educators it would have been mother, father, six sons and seven daughters. Big families were mandatory. I suppose the writers felt that an additional dozen names (per chapter) to memorize would have cluttered up the point. And I'm certainly grateful for the small families involved because the tests would have been infinitely more difficult had there been families of 15.

I have forgotten many of the illustrations but a few have survived to adulthood (or at least advanced age). Bunga was a youth who lived in the Malaya Penninsula, which is somewhere in Africa. But, because the countries have all changed their names, I don't know exactly where that is today. Of course I don't know for sure, but I'm willing to bet that Bunga has changed his name so locating him would be difficult anyway. Bunga is about the same age as I am. I know this because he was 10 when I was. When we were 10, Bunga's life consisted of running through the jungle. His father hunted with a blow gun. I don't remember his mother. Bunga wore a little something around his waist. It was always warm there so he didn't need any more for a lot of clothes. There were no illustrations of girls or women.

Bunga's life didn't seem half bad. School wasn't mentioned so Bunga must have stayed ignorant of book learning. I remember no mention of religious affiliation so I assume no missionaries had shown up.

Then there were Netsook and Claya of Alaska, which wasn't a state at that time. Now they had it rough. It was cold all the time so they wore fur parkas the year around. I believe they slept in them. There was no mention of pajamas.

Netsook and Claya lived in an igloo fashioned from frozen snow and ice. Their father hunted seals and they ate the meat and used the fur for parkas. They boiled the blubber for oil to use in their lamps. I believe that's all the stuff that was in the test.

Funny, in retrospect, the mothers seemed to keep a pretty low profile. Of course, even in this country women weren't equal then.

Patron Saints

Everybody had to have a patron saint. Usually this was the saint denoted by your first name, for example, St. Thomas if your first name is Thomas or St. James if your first name is James. Sure, you'd have a lot of people in the class claiming the same patron saint but the esteemed saint was always equal to the task of guiding his or her patrons. In addition to the standard patron saints, there were special patron saints for those who needed them.

I've forgotten some of the saints' names but I do remember that there were patron saints for slow learners, people who lost things and people who habitually disobeyed. And these patron saints would be invoked by the nuns as needed.

As an example, a nun might say: "Tommy, you pray to saint whatshisname, patron saint of dummies. See if he can help you get someplace with your arithmetic." Surprisingly, this worked a fair share of the time. I don't know if it had anything to do with the fact that if he didn't come through the nun would wipe the pupil and the patron saint off her list. I suppose in the patron saint business, how frequently you're called upon is a measure of status.

The patron saint of lost causes got prayed to a lot in my experience. As I remember, the patron saint of lost causes is St. Jude. What he did to get that distinction I don't know. But with that kind of a cause to handle he must have been busier than hell. In our school alone we had perhaps 10 to 12 people an hour praying to him.

Individuals might be required to pray to him in certain

very serious circumstances such as a high probability of failing a test and the whole class might be required to pray to him when there was an extreme problem such as a frieze behind schedule. What you have to remember is that this took place before the big purge of saints, the one that got St. Christopher and many others. St. Christopher was the patron saint of travelers and everyone was required to pray to him just before vacation or any other long car trip. I don't believe he covered airplanes. But airplane travel was so new that perhaps no patron saint had been assigned yet. A statue of St. Christopher was perched on the dash of every Catholic car. Rumor was that the good saint jumped out at 60 mph, but this was never confirmed.

Now that so many saints have been purged I doubt that there are enough left to have a separate patron for every evil and danger. Perhaps they, like parish priests, have had to double up on duties. For example, the same saint might now be handling dummies and habitual mis-creants. But I do hope they don't expect St. Jude to take on more causes. With his schedule he must be seriously overworked the way it is.

Shrines, especially to the Virgin Mary, were very popu-lar and exist even to this day. But, in the fifties, it was almost a requirement. Had nuns been permitted to travel from the convents they would have checked the home of each pupil to make sure that a shrine had been erected. If you were without a shrine to the Virgin Mary, well, it was almost like open hostility. Obviously, you and the whole family would be headed straight for hell. Yes, we had one or I wouldn't dare touch this subject.

"RUMOR WAS THAT THE GOOD SAINT JUMPED OUT
AT 60 MPH."

A shrine consisted of a large statue of the Virgin Mary usually made of plaster of Paris or plastic but plastic was just coming in so the percentage of plastic statues was low. The statue would then be placed somewhere in the yard usually near the house or by a tree. The statue might be something between 12 and 24 inches in height.

Bath tub shrines were in vogue. You took an old bath tub and buried it in the ground so that the end that came to a point was out of the ground. Depending on the size of the statue you were going to put in it, you might leave a couple of feet out of the ground. A little more or less as good taste in shrines might dictate. The statue would, therefore, be enshrined within the exposed area of the bath tub.

Medals, scapulars and holy water bottles were very popular, too. It was a rare Catholic school pupil, indeed, who didn't have an assortment of religious matter around his or her neck. A Catholic kid who did a sommersault— boy or girl—always polished off the maneuver by tucking medals and scapulars back into his or her shirt or blouse.

The small religious items—very modest in price—were obtained during periods of special devotions, such as 40-hours' devotion when such items were on sale in the hall outside the church. Also, the nuns regularly gave such items—holy cards were big—as rewards and awards.

Then there was the Catholic Christmas seal, the Holy Childhood Christmas Seal. At the same time as the widely known secular Christmas seal was being sold, Catholic grade school kids would be going door-to-door selling Holy Childhood seals: "Same price but infinitely more beneficial to your immoral (or immortal) soul; just a penny a stamp," as the sales pitch went. For nearly all Catholic families, Christmas cards bore the necessary three-cent postage stamp, the Holy Childhood Christmas seal and, if there was room and sufficient money, the standard Christmas seal.

Music was universally loved among nuns—at least the beautiful Church (read Latin) music. From first grade until the bitter end (eighth grade) music was included in the curriculum. But, since singing properly, in tune and with piety, wasn't easy for everybody, there were certain infractions related to music classes. One of the worst was stringing along. This was the practice of singing, intentionally or otherwise, a half-beat behind the rest of the class. This practice was engaged in by those who had not properly prepared for the session and, therefore, were a little uncertain of the words or melody. This was almost an inexcusable weakness because, in preparation for singing the hymn in Latin, the class would have been drilled hundreds of times over. When a hymn was introduced the nun would have us put our fingers under each note and utter the name of the note. So we'd go through perhaps a hundred dry runs, "do, re, mi, fa, fa, ti, do, do," or whatever, moving our fingers from note to note. First at a slow pace and then at a faster pace.

Then we'd sing the notes. Now singing the notes would continue until we had the rhythm and notes down pat. Only at that point—never a repetition earlier—would we proceed with the words. However, with the prior drilling, we were expected to pick up the hymn rather quickly. A couple hundred repetitions singing the words was expected to be sufficient to make our rendition acceptable to the nun.

Having been drilled us to that extent, the nun expected to have only to bleep once with her pitch pipe, raise her arms over her head and then begin waving them in proper rhythm. When her sensitive ears detected someone stringing along there was swift and stiff punishment. "Master Harmon, you're stringing along. You're making this entire hymn displeasing to God. (Automatic venial sin, at least.) You'll stay after school today and we'll see if doing the (multiplication) tables a thousand times will make you sing better from now on." I'm sure I would have had to pray to the patron saint of stringing along but I don't think there was one.

35-Minute Mass

As previously described, everyone needed to gain a full point every Sunday. Now, if time was no object you could attend the church of your choice and gain the full point in, for example, 45 minutes. But to many people, time was important so the 35-minute Sunday Mass was a popular favorite as they say in TV and radio.

Our parish had the shortest Mass around, so every Sunday Mass was crowded. It was thought by the parishoners that every shirt-tail Catholic (that is one who is just fulfilling the minimum requirements) from miles around would show up for Mass on Sunday just to get his or her full point in 35 minutes. We figured that, since we lived in the parish, we had it coming.

The two pastors who followed the one who said the

short Mass spent their tenures trying to eradicate the short-Mass reputation of the parish.

The short Mass was, nevertheless, the parish's claim to fame. Much was made in those days of belonging to the parish you lived in and properly supporting (with money) the same. The deviation of attending Mass in a neighboring parish was a widely discussed subject in theological circles. Conservative thinkers held that attending Mass in a parish other than the one you were registered in was an automatic mortal sin unless you were traveling a long way from home. Less conservative thinkers held that the same was a venial sin, provided sufficient donation was made to both parishes, the one at which you attended Mass and the one you lived in.

Whichever, the short Mass played to full houses week in and week out. The short Mass was accomplished this way. Basically, a Mass has to include the essentials to confer a full point on the attendees. But there are some optionals and the omitting of them along with the speeding up of the essentials can result in considerable time savings. The biggest time saver was a short sermon. I hate the word homily which has come to replace sermon much as the term Sacrament of Reconciliation has come to replace Confession. Both are euphemisms. Give me a good sermon anytime. A fast pass could be made through the Latin requirements because nobody understood the words anyway. Because everything except the Epistle, Gospel and sermon were said in Latin considerable time could be saved by whipping right through the Latin parts. It was proved in our parish that Latin—despite being a dead language—was not slow.

So the priest breezed right through the Latin parts and, depending on the number of people going to communion, he could have everyone out of the church—full point chalked up—in 25 to 35 minutes. The sermon was rarely more than 180 to 240 seconds. (That's three to four minutes.)

Eighth Grade Graduation

The nuns must have heaved a sigh of relief each time they graduated a batch of kids. In our school the annual number of graduates was about 80-85. Because Catholic schools went from grades one through eight (there was no junior high, per se) much was made of graduation. Though almost all went on to Catholic high school, there was great to-do about our Catholic education and our obligation as educated Catholics. Indeed, about as much was made of graduation from eighth grade as there was about high school graduation. People often sent announcements to their friends and relatives and gifts were given and received.

On the practical side, moving on to ninth grade meant splitting the sexes, something for which the nuns were eternally grateful. Each successive crop of seventh and eighth graders seemed to cause more trouble in the area of boy-girl mixing. Despite the fact that anything to do with sex was a mortal sin, the kids kept thinking about it and talking to each other. Even a conversation between an eighth grade boy and an eighth grade girl was a mortal sin if the conversation were not strictly limited to homework, saints or religious vocations.

For ninth grade and up, the nuns got the girls and

teaching priests or brothers got the boys. Nuns felt more comfortable with their classes limited to girls. There were things that they needed to pass on to them that no male should ever know about. After eighth grade, a nun almost never talked to a male. I'm not sure, but I strongly suspected that a male over the age of 14 could not be associated with (by a nun) under pain of mortal sin. If the male ever became the father of a Catholic school kid the nun could again chew him out but other than that contact was forbidden. This isn't entirely true, because nuns took great pride in their students' successes and would be delighted to talk to a former student, male or female, who was considering a religious vocation or one who had become rich and donated millions to the church.

PART II

chapter nine

High school started with ninth grade and it was the beginning of the separation of the sexes. Only boys went to this high school. A ninth grade building was located several miles from the main building because the main building, which was shortly to be expanded, couldn't hold all who attended the school. The ninth grade building was located in a residential area of the city. The neighbors probably thought that having a ninth grade boys school in the area reduced property values.

In the area in which the main building was located, it was entirely the opposite. We were the class (as in status) of the area—but that isn't saying much. The main high school building was located in an old part of the city known as The Island. It is a true island—the Mississippi River flows around a several-block area of land. The school was built on the island in the early nineteen hundreds. It's in an area that's been renovated so it isn't as slummy now as it was 20 years ago.

When I was there it was a haven for hobos—whom we

called bums. Mostly, they were just derelicts. The Island had some rundown housing, a few small businesses and the House of Charity. That was a charity started by a Catholic brother (I believe he started his own order) expressly for the purpose of serving the bums.

From some of the school windows you could see the bums lining up for their free noon lunch. One day during trigonometry class, a bum was struck by a car. I suppose I was just sitting in class day dreaming a little and looking out the window when it happened. The man must have been standing in the street when he was hit by a fast-moving car. I knew it was bad because the poor hobo was hurtled perhaps thirty feet down the street. It was the first time I'd seen a serious accident and I was sickened inside. I said my litany of "Hail Marys" and "Our Fathers" silently. All the proper emergency vehicles arrived in a short time but they took the old fella away in the coroner's vehicle, so it didn't take an intellectual heavyweight to figure out that he'd eaten his last free meal. I thought perhaps there'd be some reaction from the teacher, a lay teacher, but he never missed a word. And I just sat there wondering if I was the only one who was affected. Certainly I was not. Most of the rest of the class was pretty somber the rest of the period but the teacher kept right on with trigonometry. I learned a hell of a lot more than trigonometry that day.

Bums were generally thought to be elderly types who had fallen upon hard times. Typically, the school kids were sympathetic. (There but for the Grace of God go I someday. That was a pretty sobering thought.) We participated in school-sponsored fund-raisers for the House of Charity. I don't remember any long talks with bums but I

"IT WAS THE BEGINNING OF THE SEPARATION OF THE SEXES."

picked up a few things when they panhandled for change as we walked across the bridge to school.

Hobos were generally middle-aged to elderly. They were widely reputed to travel the rails—the tracks skirted the river's edge in front of the school—but I suspect most of them really lived in the island area and never got farther than the adjacent downtown business area in which they begged for money.

It was obvious that most of them suffered from the demon booze. And we joked that the price of a cup of coffee for which they incessantly pleaded came surprisingly close to the cost of a bottle of cheap wine. The bum usually tried to convince you that he was a big tipper if you asked why he needed 30 cents for a cup of coffee that cost a dime at the local diner. The diner on The Island, by the way, was off limits for the high school kids. We were repeatedly reminded of this but the cafe seemed to do a good business among the high school kids, anyway.

The students typically came from large families which probably had more than a couple of kids in local Catholic schools. The tuition, books and cost of public transportation added to enough to make sure that most of the school kids weren't that much better off financially than the bums. So, as a rule, I don't think the vagabonds did that well off of us but there were a few times I felt a donation was wise. This was usually when I was alone and not feeling very confident. One day on my way across the bridge (the city bus ended its run four or five blocks from the school) a younger looking bum approached me from the opposite direction. Younger bums—those in the fortyish vicinity—were physically more imposing than the tottering older ones. Anyway, when he stopped me he dug in his pocket and simultaneously inquired if I'd like to buy a razor.

Before I saw the razor I had my mind made up to buy it. I envisioned it as a straight-edge type which might come dangerously close to a vein if I wasn't pleasant about the whole thing. It turned out to be a well worn safety razor instead of the straight edge I'd pictured in my mind. I didn't take the razor. I sort of made the two-bits a down payment on the thing.

Tricks played on hobos were regularly told but seldom did I see a trick in progress. I think I saw the end of this one. A couple of kids in the class got possession of an empty gin bottle, certainly no difficult task because they were dropped by bums in whatever spot they were in when the last drop was drained. The kids filled it with clear vinegar. They proceeded to sell it to a bum. Before he could get the top off the kids were running like hell. The two bragged about it around the school for days.

Smoking among the school students was considered to be a big problem in those days. Therefore, smoking was prohibited anywhere on the island. Quite frequently, kids were caught smoking. It was sort of the "in" thing to do— get caught smoking, that is. The penalty was reputed to be death but nobody lost his life over smoking.

At the building that was maintained for the ninth grad-ers, which was several miles from the main building so there was no association between the ninth graders and the older kids, incoming students got their first taste of high school. The building was a former public elementary school and the yard was not entirely suited to the physical needs of 14 and 15 year-old boys. The small school yard was partitioned into four or five softball diamonds and outfields overlapped. The distance from homeplate (positioned near the perimeter sidewalk) to the school building was too short for home run hitters so we played a softball-like game which we called mushball. The game balls were doctored by the brothers, I assume, so that they were almost mushy. The brothers must have used sponges in place of the standard softball core. Still there was an occasional broken window. The really strong kids could put the ball against the building "on a line," that is, hard enough to break a window if it hit one. The rest of the kids could pop it up so that on the way down it would weakly brush the window or building.

Like attending a Catholic grade school, attending a Catholic high school was almost mandatory. Nowadays, people make a conscious decision to attend a Catholic school with viable options considered. In those days, if a good Catholic family felt it needed to send a child or children to a public school, the parents sought a dispensation from the parish priest. Depending on the priest, the questions as to financial situation might be very probing or quite superficial. It was assumed that the only reason parents wouldn't send their kids to a Catholic high school was a lack of financial ability. It was understood by even the least sophisticated that you didn't drive to the rectory in a new car or wear a new suit when you were on the mission of seeking a dispensation. Any sign of affluence could hurt your chances.

In cases of real financial need, the parish priest, it is

reputed, found ways, possibly from parish funds, to see that the kid's tuition got paid. The high schools were not directly connected with the parishes but it was not unusual for parishes which sent large numbers of pupils to a Catholic high school to have a working relationship that included a contribution from the parish. The grade schools were run by the parishes so the parish priest had firm and direct control. But the high schools were usually run by the teaching order that staffed the school or by the diocese.

Attending a Catholic high school really included more than just financial sacrifice. Typically, the Catholic school was not as close to home as the public school. So many kids took public buses to and from school, a one-way distance of 10 miles or more in many cases. In addition to the direct cost, there was the time factor and the bus schedule. The bus rides might add as much as two hours a day, an hour on each side, to the school session. And the bus schedules were such that after-school social gatherings might put you beyond the last bus home. Since it was just as difficult to get back to the school for evening events, such as basketball games, school relationships became limited to the class day.

Catholic high schools then were geared to preparation for college. Vocational skills weren't taught. There weren't facilities. And the students' choices of curriculum were limited, indeed. For that matter, your counselor made the choice for you. I suppose if you really wanted to argue and maybe bring your parents into it, you might have effected a change but I don't remember that happening. The system was rigid and the counselor served 1,000 boys so extensive deliberations were not commonplace.

Typically, the result of the system was a well educated graduate. No deviation from the standard result was allowed. Because there were kids waiting to get in, if you didn't meet the standard you could be banished to a public school. Though, typically, expulsions were for disciplinary reasons rather than academic.

It was widely reputed in secular circles that the Catholic schools reveled in semi-stupid louts who could play football. Too dumb to graduate, they would play football forever. But that didn't happen much, that I knew of. Kids had to take an entrance test so there was little likelihood that a person of less than minimum intellectual credentials would get in in the first place. It was true, however, that Catholic high schools got 100 percent of the talented Catholic athletes. Catholic school interscholastic athletic teams were generally high caliber, or as much so as limited facilities would permit.

The schools athletic standouts, past and present, were held up as heroes, especially if they were academically superior also. We were all expected to motivate ourselves to be like them.

The expansive and inclusive Catholic high school systems eliminated (or at least reduced to a bare minimum) the necessity to interface with public schools and public school students. Catholic grade schools and high schools had their own academic and sports arenas. Indeed, little if any contact was made in the field of athletic endeavor and little more in the area of academic endeavor. The organization that governed public school athletics specifically prohibited competition between its member schools and private schools, not just Catholic schools.

Because Catholic schools did get almost all the top-notch Catholic athletes, Catholic school sports teams generally were of equal or better caliber than public school teams. A Catholic boys high school of 1,000 certainly had a numerical advantage on almost all public schools of the area.

Indeed, it was in the area of interscholastic sports competition that the barriers were the last to crumble. In the early seventies, when the private schools were finally admitted to the public school body that regulated sports, it was at a point in time when the private schools, Catholic in particular, were losing enrollment. The original reason for not permitting private schools to participate with public schools was that the private schools were not limited to students from a particular area as were public schools which drew students from within a defined boundary. Private schools, therefore, could recruit students from any area of the city.

chapter ten

Just as describing a nun (without benefit of a photo) was a challenge, so is describing a teaching brother. Christian Brothers, abundant in number in those days, staffed several boys high schools in the area. There seemed to be many who talked of the way it was in Chicago so I got the impression that the order was perhaps based or at least started in that area. Drawing on the parallel with priests, one can cover a lot of ground in the area of describing a teaching brother. The brothers' black cassock is exactly like that of a priest. It covers the teaching brother from neck to ankle. Beneath the cassock a brother wore black trousers—again just like a priest. There was no way to tell by looking whether or not a shirt was worn beneath the cassock. A shirt would, however, seem entirely unnecessary.

The way to tell a priest from a brother is the collar. The standard Roman collar of a priest was changed to distinguish the brothers. Instead of a little rectangular opening in front (the standard Roman collar), the brothers' collar had a white cardboard-like protrusion, rectangular in shape, originating in the area below the chin. It stuck out in front about six inches and was split up the middle. It had sort of a vague resemblance to a bow tie—a stiff, white bow tie.

The function of the collar is something I can't even take a good guess at. I'm sure it wasn't entirely comfortable and therefore might have been thought of as a penance by those who designed it.

Because the entire head showed there was no mistaking that brothers were males. And they had male names. There were nuns named Sister Harvey Joe but no brothers named Brother Mary Margaret (that I heard of, anyway).

A brother would be addressed as Brother Charles or Brother James or maybe just brother. But there was no accepted way of shortening brother as there was sister into 'ster. To my knowledge "bro" was never used.

Brothers came pretty much in all shapes and sizes and even ages. Again, because the entire head was visible, brothers had ages. Not known in years, of course, but relative—young, middle aged, old and very old. Gray hair distinguished young from old. The very old were revered by the other brothers and the high school students and respect was accorded them by all.

Brothers never talked of childhood, but mother and father were mentioned once in a while. This is in contrast to nuns who never mentioned other members of their family. Brothers talked extensively of prior classes in this school and others which were always much smarter, harder working and more accomplished in athletics.

Because high school-age boys were just a little less under the thumb of their parents, brothers didn't use their influence with parents as extensively as the nuns did in grade school. Occasionally, they'd link you and your behavior to that of an older brother or even father as two or three generations of boys attending the school was not uncommon. Usually this connection was made in a negative sense such as, "your brother was a screw-off just like you. I don't know how he made it through here. We must have been softer then. If you want to take after him and be a failure, too, just keep doin' what you're doin'. We can have you in a public school this afternoon if you don't shape up."

The brothers typically used reverse psychology, too. Such as: "I know you can't do it. I've been watching you for three years now and I've got you figured. You're the kind that lucks out in a test once in a while but, when the chips are down, you goof it up."

Brothers lived a celibate life but, unlike nuns, they were known to enjoy some of the pleasures of secular life. Nuns never appeared in public except in big groups and nuns were never seen eating. Indeed, I doubt that nuns were even allowed soft drinks in private. Brothers were just a little less restricted. Brothers could drink beer in private and play golf. A beer truck made a stop at the brothers' residence (adjacent to the school) about once a week. This isn't intended to imply that there was any excess only that drinking beer was not, per se, unacceptable for the brothers.

A game of golf on Saturday was acceptable, too. I

believe it was mentioned in passing by certain brothers than an occasional golf course operator would be predisposed toward allowing brothers free use of the facilities.

Indeed, most brothers had a hobby. One brother loved buses and took great pride in keeping the school's bus (which was probably his) in mint condition inside and out—moving parts and non-moving parts.

Brothers are not priests and therefore cannot say Mass or hear confessions or perform any other duties specifically limited to priests. Their vocation in this order was to teach high school boys. And that they did with vigor. They wanted their classes to be the best. There was no place for second-best.

At that time there was not an abundance of teaching brothers but there were sufficient numbers to staff the high schools in much the same way that nuns staffed the grade schools. There would be a lay teacher or two or maybe a half-dozen in a high school. I'd say 10-25 percent lay teachers was about the average. A lay teacher in a Catholic boys high school was always male. Indeed, the only females on campus were an office woman and a cook—both matronly types. Usually, lay teachers were fatherly types but occasionally there was a young lay teacher. Typically, a lay teacher could teach any subject for which he was qualified except religion, which was the province of the brothers.

Not long after my period in Catholic high schools, brothers began to leave the orders and there were fewer

"WE CAN HAVE YOU IN PUBLIC SCHOOL THIS AFTERNOON
IF YOU DON'T SHAPE UP."

coming in. So ample numbers became a problem. I assume that brothers had less trouble than ex-nuns in acclimating to the secular world because the brothers had at least some contact with it during their "hitch."

Brothers never went out of their way to give students the impression that they (the students) were human or anything. But the brothers did let it be known that they were proud of their successful students. "Easy Ed" Mac-auley, a professional basketball player of the era, was spoken of frequently. Ed was a product of a school run by the brothers and Easy Ed made it big in the pro game. Many brothers had fond stories of Easy Ed. It was pointed out, too, that Ed made the sign of the cross before every free throw attempt. And, as evidence that this was a pretty good practice, it was pointed out that Ed had one of the best free throw percentages in the league.

Brothers could be recognized as fat or thin or some-where between. Some brothers had vibrant personalities and some were almost somber. A few showed a genuine liking for their students. And I think all had a deep concern for the welfare of the students. Like nuns, broth-ers talked mostly about prior classes and prior teaching assignments and rarely about family or friends. I assume most young males made the decision to become a brother at a very young age—often early teens—and part of the conditioning process in becoming a brother (as it is with nuns and priests, too) is to eradicate any ties with family and friends.

A popular misconception at that time was that brothers were priest-aspirants who didn't quite make the grade.

This was patently untrue but the misconception wasn't generally dignified by denial.

Brothers lived in a community like nuns. And, as each community of nuns had a mother superior, each community of brothers had a head brother. Brothers could be freer about appearing in public than nuns. Still brothers did not associate much outside of their own community.

The ignominy of the era was to be thrown out of the Catholic high school. Because there were kids waiting to get in, the school really didn't need you. So sometimes they made good in their threats to kick somebody out. However, it was really quite rare. I think there were fewer than a half-dozen kids who left the school in my four-year tenure. And that would be for all reasons including moving out of the area, financial and disciplinary. In most cases I suspect that the kids who withdrew did so by mutual consent of student, parents and school administrators.

The rules of the school were more in keeping with older kids than say the rules of grade schools. There wasn't, for instance, a ban on talking in the lavatory. Fortunately or unfortunately, most of the kids came from Catholic grade schools and talking in the lavatory had been foreign to their existence for so many years that few developed the practice in high school.

There was a dress code. You had to wear dress pants (no jeans which weren't as popular then anyway); a shirt with a collar (that ruled out tee shirts); and shoes that could be shined (that eliminated tennis shoes). I suspect that if a tie were still the rule of the day (ties had been dropped from the dress code several years earlier) every-one would have complied. By accident or by design, the code didn't specify how long any one outfit might be worn and there were those who looked like they wore the same clothes from September through May.

Some Catholic high schools required uniforms so per-haps we were fortunate. But there might have been some thought put into that, too. Our school served a less than affluent area of the city and uniforms might have been the straw that broke the camel's financial back for some families.

The strictest rules I remember were those that related to attendance and staying on the school grounds. Those kinds of rules must have been pretty much universal at the time because even the public school kids had to abide by rules of this type.

On The Hour And On The Half Hour

Praying was something we did quite a bit of. It was standard to offer some fairly lengthy prayers at the begin-ning and end of the school day. The longer session was at the outset of classes. We had a relatively short prayer that was said at the beginning of each class period. It was that one that occurred pretty much on the hour.

We had a brief prayer that was to be said on the half hour. The prayer on the half hour wasn't always remem-bered by the teacher because there was no automatic reminder built into the system. Still, it was typical that the teacher would notice the half-hour point and we'd bow our heads and recite the brief prayer.

It wasn't a consuming religious atmosphere. I don't remember being hampered by religious content. On rare occasions, we had a Mass said in the school, with a priest from a nearby parish invited to do the honors. We had no real chapel so the gymnasium was used for this purpose. While most of my memories of these occasions have been replaced by more recent experiences, I do remember that a few hundred young males singing hymns—specifically "Holy God We Praise Thy Name"—is a beautiful experience. Indeed, even more beautiful sung acappella, which was standard for us.

chapter eleven

Homeroom, changing rooms for different classes and many other daily affairs were new to ninth graders coming out of Catholic grade schools. For better or for worse, about 40 of us drew room 210, known as "210, The-Room-For-Men," and its reigning king, Brother Fastidius. Brother Fastidius changed his name a couple of years later for reasons never made public. (It couldn't have been creditors so it must have been that St. Fastidius was failing to come through in the clutch so the good brother had no choice but to seek another, more successful patron saint.) A short time after I graduated, I heard that he left the order. I suppose that the second patron saint also failed.

Brother Fastidius hated mediocrity with a passion. He's the one who christened room 210 the room for men. We were 14-year-old men and we didn't take that lightly. Brother Fastidius hated second place in anything. We were to be first in any competition between classes and first even when there wasn't any competition.

He once told us that the worst thing somebody could say about you was that you meant well. I spent years reflecting on that. My interpretation (he never interpreted the comment for us) was that while the remark might be intended to soothe your feelings it is an obvious indication that you have failed in your objective. You don't have to say "he meant well" when the guy succeeds—only when he fails.

Brother Fastidius didn't think small. And he didn't ever consider an alternative to complete achievement of the objective, whatever it was. So when it came to the annual fund-raising drive—magazine subscription sales—he ordered that room 210 should win and win by a wide margin. It might even be undesirable to win by a small margin because that would indicate that your opponents had a chance to win.

And win we did. The prize was sufficient money to buy food for a picnic and the use of the school bus to get to the picnic site.

Keeping tuition as low as possible was vital to Catholic schools. For a while in the fifties tuition was $175 per school year per student. And it might even have ratcheted downward for additional kids from the same family. So fund raising was (and is) a way of Catholic school life.

The biggest fund-raiser at that time was the magazine drive. It annually raised several thousand dollars for the school. Typically, the ninth graders did the best. The drive was new to them and people have more compassion for a 14-year-old than an 18-year-old. The year I was in ninth grade, room 210 had gross sales of over $6,000. One kid—

a super salesman—could sell subscriptions to the illiterate.

Brother Fastidius didn't take kindly to anybody who didn't excel at magazine sales. I, and a very few others, didn't and we weren't exactly drawn into his favor. Like everyone else, I tried to sell magazine subscriptions. It was good experience if for no other reason than to find out the many and various ways people can say "no." I hit my friends and relatives and even bought subscriptions to a couple of magazines myself. But I certainly never hit the respectable list among the salesmen of room 210.

Door-to-door sales just didn't yield any success. I was skunked. I probably started out my sales pitch : "you don't want to buy any magazine subscriptions, do you?" Close neighbors almost slammed the door in my face. I know I was doing something wrong. My failure notwithstanding, room 210 was the clear winner of the sales competition. So we took the money and brother Fastidius bought 45 T-bone steaks and neccessary condiments and we used the school bus to have our picnic at a site about 90 miles from the school. It was the first time I, and probably many others, had eaten T-bone steak.

Mr. Grutchnik

Mr. Grutchnik was a geometry teacher of European extraction who was anything but conventional. Indeed, he is a rich source of anecdotes—all exactly portrayed here without embellishment. The only change is his name which intentionally is not genuine. I don't want him to be able to sue. Short of fuse and direct of action, Mr. Grutchnik perpetrated some painful but memorable experiences.

In a tenth grade plane geometry class that he taught, a member of the class aroused Mr. Grutchnik's ire through incessant fooling around and talking. I hadn't noticed the infraction or infractions but then I was inclined to stay involved in my own. (You've heard the old saying: "mind your own infractions.") Mr. Grutchnik called the offender to the front of the class and failed to inform him of his rights, which was common in those days because students were widely held to have signed away their rights on the application for enrollment. After requiring the offender to sit atop a high stool facing the rest of the class, Mr. Grutchnik withdrew from his desk drawer a roll of wide adhesive tape—the type of tape a football coach uses to tape his players legs and ankles.

Without further ado, Mr. Grutchnik ordered the miscreant to extend his arms in front of him with wrists together. With the flair of a maestro, Mr. Grutchnik wrapped the offenders' wrists securely. Then, taking care to allow respiration through the nose, the colorful teacher wrapped the two-inch wide tape around the miscreant's head precluding anything louder than a deep breath.

That took care of the offender. He didn't make a sound the rest of the class period. I don't suppose he learned much about geometry that day but there's something educational about silence, even if it's forced.

Mr. Grutchnik was not unjustly inclined to single people out for punishment. When the situation dictated, he could be judiciously fair and equitable. In one such case he got us all. As was common in his class, there was a considerable amount of individual work. Mr. Grutchnik would make an assignment which each of us would undertake. Then he would move about the room observing progress and helping those who required it. It was a good technique because it tended to benefit those who needed help and it served the needs of those who could catch on without individual help.

It did have one considerable weakness: it prevented Mr. Grutchnik from keeping his eyes on everybody. And there were those who could not pass up the opportunity for some minor—but stimulating—mischief.

One bright spring day of pleasant temperature with the windows open wide, we were in the student-tutor syndrome. Mr. Grutchnik was tutoring a student attempting an assignment which included lengthy writing of theorems on the chalkboard. With teacher and student facing the chalkboard, there was opportunity for others in the class to pursue some much needed enjoyment. Anyway, the guy, who sat behind the student being helped at the chalkboard, reached forward, grabbed his classmate's text and sailed it out the window frisbee style.

When the kid finished his private session and returned to his desk he naturally became curious as to what had happened to his geometry book. Pretty soon Mr. Grutchnik noticed the kid's wonderment and inquired into the situation. Soon kids and teacher were peering out the window at the geometry book on the sidewalk two floors down.

Mr. Grutchnik began inquiring of others, first the student who sat behind the one who lost the book. Indeed, he was the offender but he was of insufficient moral fiber to admit the deed. The miscreant falsely indicated an absolute ignorance of the way the book had come to find its way to the sidewalk. So Mr. Grutchnik ordered the party whom he'd just interrogated to remove all his belongings from the desk. This included texts for a bunch of classes, notebooks and other assorted papers. Then the teacher sent the belongings sailing out the window in much the same manner as the student had done with the text book. As the notebooks and loose papers were buffeted by the springtime breeze they began to drift and scatter like fall leaves. All the pained student could do was watch his coveted notes and essays drop out of sight.

Continuing at the row nearest the window, Mr. Grutchnik proceeded to inquire of each individual and as each pleaded ignorant and innocent Mr. Grutchnik tossed the contents of the kid's desk out the window.

Seated several rows from the window, I had time to consider ways of minimizing my losses. So I removed all but a couple of texts from my desk and trapped the most valuable of my possessions between my knees and the underside of my desk. When Mr. Grutchnik got to me— perhaps the thirtieth kid—I was set. First I played my best card. Offering a few token texts on the top of my desk, I responded to his inquiries with protestations of ignorance and innocence. The former he conceded and the latter he disputed. But, with less than a firm conviction to refrain from being a fink, I asked Mr. Grutchnik if I would be spared should I divulge the identity of the perpetrator. "No," he said and raked the token texts from my desk top. Soon they too were in the growing heap of books on the sidewalk.

"ALL THE PAINED STUDENT COULD DO WAS WATCH HIS COVETED
NOTES AND ESSAYS DROP OUT OF SIGHT."

I was feeling successful with the majority of my belongings safely between my knees and the underside of my
desk when the kid behind me "finked." Immediately Mr.
Grutchnik returned, forced me to surrender the
remainder of my belongings and hurled them out the
window. Just before the irritated teacher concluded the
task of throwing everybody's stuff out the window, an
aging brother who had apparently gotten wind of the
bookstorm shuffled through the door and asked what the
hell was going on. Mr. Grutchnik, still tossing things out
the window, didn't tender a response. Startled, the brother stared momentarily in silence and then ordered us to
reclaim our stuff. As I recall, we had to wait for the period-
ending bell before going out to get our stuff, some of
which was never to be found.

It was another of those times when Mr. Grutchnik was
offering individual help that my pencil became dull. I was
drawing cartoons and a sharp pencil is nearly essential.
So I went to the front of the room where the sharpener was
located and accomplished what I set out to do. Pencil
sharpening was permitted under these circumstances so I
had committed no violations—venial or mortal. But on
the way back to my desk I stopped near the teacher's
position and just did a short pantomime. Mr. Grutchnik
was facing the other way. My little act was nothing special, nothing very creative. Just a little arm waving and lip
moving perhaps of 10 seconds duration.

Back at my desk, I bent over so my head was just a few
inches from the desk top and continued drawing my
cartoon. The next thing I knew my head was rebounding
from the desk top. Mr. Grutchnik had snuck up behind me

and rapped me on the back of my head with his text book. I concluded, when my head cleared, that he had been offended by my pantomime. I had a consuming headache the rest of the day and I never seriously pursued the performing arts after that.

Latin Class

Latin was losing favor as the language of the church about this time but as an academic pursuit—indeed, a required academic pursuit—it hung on for years. If you didn't have a good excuse, you were going to take two years of Latin. As a requirement to graduate from high school, the state required two years of a foreign language, which suited the Catholic high school administrators perfectly. The church had always had this huge majority of people who didn't understand the Latin prayers of the Mass and, worse than that, they botched the pronunciation of the responses. Latin classes—fully endorsed by the state—gave the Catholic academicians an opportunity to eradicate that weakness.

So almost everyone took two years of Latin. Most of the time we were learning something, if not Latin. For example, in our sophomore Latin class we soon learned that the teacher didn't go to great lengths to check our homework translations. We discovered that if we translated the first couple of paragraphs, we could just write the rest of the assignment in its native Latin and get credit for the work.

I'm living proof that this technique—harmful as it is to the learning of Latin—can come back to haunt you. Other parts of the class weren't as easy to fake. The situations in which we'd be called upon to translate aloud fell into the category of being impossible to fake. Usually, with a few smarts you could buy yourself some time. The teacher would establish an order and each kid would translate a paragraph. You could then determine which paragraph you'd have to translate and work like crazy on it until your turn came.

Translating aloud really separated the men from the boys and I got separated a time or two. One time—I don't remember if I was surprised by being called on out of turn or whether I was just incompetent—I drew a blank when I looked at the passage I was required to translate. Of course, each passing second seemed like hours. Everyone was waiting for me—except, perhaps, the kids who hadn't translated yet and were probably working feverishly on their parts. But it seemed like everybody was waiting for me and the silence was deafening.

Fortunately, in a few seconds something did come to me. The passage started out "quoque Albanius" or something like that and I knew that "alb" was "white" and "quoque" meant "also." So I said "They were also white" and regretted my translation immediately. The whole class broke into roaring laughter. Mercifully, the teacher passed my paragraph on to the next kid who came closer with something about the Albanians.

The Latin teacher did have a little trouble controlling the troops. Most of what went on under his nose was just good clean fun and nobody was hurt. One of the kids in the class—not one who was not particularly a trouble-maker but one who did like to have a little fun—would begin any recitation or response to the teacher with a long "gnow." It was just sort of a nasal sound he made like the word "now" with a "g" in front. It was nonsensical and harmless. But the teacher must have figured the student had some sort of speech impediment because he'd just stand there with a blank look on his face and the kid would shortly get into that which he was supposed to be reciting. As the kid explained on occasion outside earshot of the teacher "gnow" was just a little disrespectful interjection that he put in because he could get by with it. Instead of saying "Mr. So-and-so" he used "gnow."

One time while innocently studying Latin I was a victim of mistaken identification and got bopped about the head and shoulders a few times. I'm not bitter about it at all, but for the life of me, I can't figure how I could have been picked out of class in which everybody looked alike—sort of tall, very skinny, and wearers of glasses. Anyway, as we were leaving the class, someone (unknown to me) hawked up a good goober and let fly out the window. (That is to say, someone spit out the window.) Probabilities are that it innocuously hit the sidewalk a floor below but it upset the elderly brother who was in charge of attendance and between-class behavior.

Anyway, the elderly brother, at least 80 years old at the time but 10 years from the end of his reign, grabbed me from the hoard changing classes and worked me over about the head and shoulders. He was fully six inches shorter (maybe more) and, because of his advanced age, he'd long since ceased to be physically punishing (if he confined himself to his bare hands). But he even worked over the biggest and meanest of football players. And to a man, they humbly submitted and exhibited what looked like evidence of genuine physical pain. I considered it an act of ultimate respect for the aging brother that not one of these hulks would humiliate the old man by indicating that he wasn't hurting them.

I was being marched to the elderly brother's office to await punishment which would certainly have been more painful than that already administered when the actual culprit—dry of mouth, I assume—was apprehended.

chapter twelve

To say that all of us who took American History in 10th grade were deeply religious would be a distortion of fact. There were, however, certain desecrations that even the worst among us wouldn't contemplate. And one was to deny a request made by the Virgin Mary.

A male lay teacher who generally taught ninth graders had to substitute for our regular history teacher one day. And, as generally was the case, the class tested the new teacher—a short, frail-looking man in his early fifties. He obviously abhorred violence. How he chose teaching in a boys high school escapes my imagination.

Halfway through the period the decibel level in the room reached that of a rock concert. Well, maybe not quite that level, but loud at any rate. Admonitions by the teacher to restore quiet caused only further uproar.

The teacher faced the class shaking and nearly in tears. Indeed, I'm sure I saw real tears. Most of the teachers—

brothers certainly and most of the lay teachers—would have threatened violence sufficient to reduce all of us to scraps of flesh and bone and some would have given us just enough of a taste to make us believers. But then most of these men were bigger and definitely meaner than this man.

As if finally possessed of a solution, the teacher walked to the corner of the room where a statue of the Virgin Mary was resting on a pedestal. There in front of the statue he knelt to pray and silence pervaded the room in seconds. The teacher continued his prayer for a moment, stood and resumed his lecture. As I recall, the silence lasted the remainder of the period.

The brother who taught trigonometry and other mathematics courses to the juniors and seniors was reputed to be brilliant. But he preferred seeing as little of the students as possible. His lectures were usually well above the brightest among us. Often he would be lecturing from the deepest recesses of his brain, strolling subconsciously about the front of the room, occasionally stopping and closing his eyes to ponder a particularly deep point. On some occasions, he'd be lecturing as he strolled right out of the room. A few minutes later, he would return still lecturing.

He, on his better days, allowed for questions. But on his poorer days, he treated questions with great contempt. So if you felt compelled to ask him something, you tried to pick a good spot. Mostly, it was better to ask one of the brighter guys. If one of them didn't know, everybody was going to miss it on the test anyway.

Though vocations to the religious life were encouraged through all the Catholic school years, efforts seemed to peak during the early high school period. To say that there was extreme pressure to consider a vocation would not be entirely true, but to say that vocations weren't stressed would not be true either. There was considerable attention paid to vocations—assignments in the area of what we wanted to be when we grew up, special vocation-week activities and things of that sort. Vocations were talked about from the earliest grades through high school.

Those who displayed an interest were given the opportunity to consider the call as early as ninth grade. Prior to that time, the idea was nurtured but the kid stayed in his family environment. At the tender age of 13 or 14 (ninth grade) boys or girls could be carried off to convents and seminaries never to be seen again by friends and only rarely by relatives. Once the 14-year-old had made the commitment, the system assured that little was done to interfere with it. Very little contact outside the cloister was allowed. Parents were permitted infrequent visits on the grounds and trips home were even less frequent. Then, while at home, the religious-in-training was not allowed to participate in anything secular. Parents, brothers and sisters soon grew to think of their kin as a far off relative. It was just assumed that the kid made the right decision and nobody should challenge it.

When I was a ninth grader we had a boy recruited to be a brother. For purposes of this portrayal I'll call him Eddie, even though that isn't his real name. I knew Eddie because I had gone to grade school with him. We hadn't been particularly close but we did associate and had he and his family moved out of state or something I would have expected that he would have given his classmates advance notice and there would have been a round of "goodbyes."

It was into the fall of our ninth grade year when Eddie disappeared. He was 14, I assume, though it is possible that he would have reached his fifteenth birthday. Eddie was a pretty good athlete and a little mischievous but generally on the good side of average.

Anyway, I noticed his absence and began to ask around. I don't know how long he'd been gone, perhaps a few days. Some checking yielded the rumor that he'd gone off to the brothers' training center. And this was fact I learned much later.

I was surprised that no particular mention was made of his recruitment. I would have thought it beneficial to future recruitment to at least make some mention of each person who left the school to take up the religious life. Apparently, the hierarchy felt it was risky to give the situation notice which might lead to second thoughts by the recruit.

I don't remember a member of the faculty making reference to Eddie going off to study to be a brother and I don't remember talk among the school kids or parish kids. It was just accepted. God got another one. It was accepted that a person of 14 or 15 was ready to make a decision of that finality. It is purported by church hierarchy that there is ample opportunity to change one's mind. However, it is as much of a certainty that any contacts with the outside world which might lead to that changing of the mind were precluded.

To give this situation perspective, very few were recruited out of our school, which included about 1,000 boys mostly from working-class families. Eddie was the only boy from that year's class to be recruited successfully, at least the only one that I knew of. In the next three years, a few more drifted off but some returned after a short trial.

'Because sex was expressly forbidden, just about anything that had to do with the body was forbidden. One took a shower looking at the shower head so as not to inadvertently see himself or another if it were a community shower, as is the case in locker rooms.

One day when we arrived for our 11th grade civics class, a typical jock strap or athletic supporter, if you prefer, was hanging from one of the overhead pipes. It was a basement classroom and the heat and plumbing pipes were exposed but painted. As the class members filed into the room and noticed the jock, some laughing and tittering took place mostly because it was an unusual place to see one. Remember we were all males including the teacher and we wore the things so it didn't seem like a big deal to me. But the teacher—a lay teacher in his late twenties or early thirties—nearly came unglued. We got a lecture instead of our usual civics class that day.

Absence of Girls

Some contact between the sexes was allowed in the last

year or so of high school. But the relationship between boys and girls was pretty well stifled by the years of no contact so, on the average, there was little except imagination to comfort the boys. I assume the same situation prevailed for a high percentage of the girls who attended Catholic girls schools. Girls from neighboring Catholic schools (non-Catholics would not be invited) might be invited to a sock hop after a basketball game, for instance. That would guarantee a long line, maybe a double-line, of boys on one side of the gym and a short line of girls on the other. As I recall, ninth and tenth grade boys were not allowed to attend.

Maybe—just maybe—after 90 minutes or so of musing, the gutsier of the boys (or girls) might work up the courage to establish verbal communication with a member of the opposite sex. Then you could damn well bet that the sock hop would be over before the situation could spread widely. Maybe that didn't happen as much by design as by accident, but it certainly seemed to be more than coincidence.

So for the most part girls were done without. Sure, you saw them on the street and working in various places so it was impossible to ignore their existence, but rarely did you actually speak to one.

If you stop to think about it, almost anyplace where girls or women are desirable, you can get along with a male if you have to. You were reading carefully, I hope. I said "almost anyplace." A few examples: females were desirable as cheerleaders but the principal of the nearest Catholic girls school (Sister Wayne St. Chastity) ruled that cheerleading wasn't ladylike. All that jumping around with so much skin showing was bound to excite the starving natives. And she was this wise probably never having heard of pent-up demand.

Therefore we had male cheerleaders. This could have been a real problem had we played schools with female cheerleaders. But, because all the Catholic schools were in the same boat and because we competed only with other Catholic school teams, the problem never had to be faced.

Girls might be imported for the school play if there were parts for which girls were essential. A boy could take the part of an old woman, for instance, but there were still certain roles for which a girl was definitely essential. Therefore a handful of girls would be imported from a nearby Catholic girls high school. The boys school then reciprocated for plays at the girls school. Because the numbers exchanged were small, school administrators on both sides could screen the aspirants carefully to weed out the boys who drooled in the presence of girls and the girls who smiled seductively in the presence of boys.

Perhaps even back then the hazards of a male homecoming queen were recognized, because it was standard practice to have a female homecoming queen. Lacking females in the school, the situation necessitated a procedure of advancing homecoming queen candidates via black-and-white (mug-shot type) photographs. Indeed, some of the photographs might have been taken in those booths in which you can get four poses for a quarter. The candidates were supposed to come from among the girl friends, sisters and other female relatives of the guys in the school.

Photos were posted on a bulletin board. Sure, somebody usually put up the centerfold from one of the girlie magazines but I assume all votes for that candidate were sent to a handwriting analyst to ferret out the degenerates.

Votes were tallied and the winner announced. No big deal, same picture before the voting as after. I never met a homecoming queen in person but I figured God wanted it that way. Pictures can't walk down a runway to the tune of "Here She Comes . . ." and we didn't have any Bert Parks anyway. So the hoopla around the naming of the homecoming queen lacked zest. It was more like watching election returns than a homecoming queen selection but it was the best we had.

This process of nominating and selecting a homecoming queen did have its drawbacks. Photos just don't tell everything. Especially mug-shot photographs.

Had I seen the candidates in person I might have changed my vote. But, really, this isn't of tremendous consequence. We were not a difficult audience to please. I think I can speak for the entire student body when I say I never met a homecoming queen candidate that I didn't like.

I'm sure the Catholic school administrators lamented the tradition of homecoming queens because it threatened the spiritual well-being of the students—boys and girls.

Not having girls in the school made it easy in some ways. For one, the school didn't have to have air-tight locker rooms. There was a large accordian-style door to shut off the locker room from the main hallway of the school but it was never closed during regular classes. So when a guy finished his shower he just walked out to his locker, which was in the hallway, dried and put on his clothes. Typically, the only other people around would be those in the particular gym class and if there were others walking the hallways between classes they'd not be offended by a partially clothed classmate.

However, there was some potential danger. Outsiders might be roaming the hallway unaware. One day some girls from a nearby Catholic (or public) school cut classes to roam the hallways at our school. They were pleased, I'm sure, to coming across guys emerging from the shower in their nakedness and others only slightly more pro- tected. The girls squealed and ran out the back door. It was never confirmed that they ran out the back door but the squealing I can verify as a first hand witness.

In first through eighth grades, Catholic school boys and girls attended classes together and the texts showed males and females, usually mother, father and offspring. In ninth grade when boys went to boys schools and girls to girls schools, texts used in the boys school were devoid of females. Save for statues of the Virgin Mary and two or three matronly women, you could go through a school year without seeing a female. Because doing secretarial things was women's work, the brothers always had a matronly woman to work in the school office. And there might be two or three women who cooked the school

"I NEVER MET A HOMECOMING QUEEN CANDIDATE I DIDN'T LIKE."

lunches. Typically, mothers of the students provided as much of the labor as possible in this area.

Texts rarely indicated the presence of women in the world. It all seemed normal at the time. The students were males, teachers were males and everyone else you came in contact with at the school was male. Were it not for the traditions of homecoming queen and school plays, there would have been no need whatsoever for females.

Horror Stories

I didn't witness this one, but the brother who told it swore it was true. He said that when he was teaching at another school (certainly not ours), he had a boy in class who paid no particular attention to personal hygiene so he smelled pretty bad. Of course, the rest of the kids in the class and the teacher didn't like it but there wasn't much they could do. One day one of the kids offered the opinion that the kid smelled worse than a goat. It must have been a rural school. Pretty soon there was some wagering going on. Perhaps a few with olfactory impairment wagered on the goat smelling worse. It so happened that one of the kids was able to secure a goat for the test.

Next the goat was brought in to the class for a side-by-side comparison. After several minutes of sniffing there was apparent division among the class as to which smelled worse, the kid or the goat. Several more minutes of discussion failed to resolve the dispute and just when it appeared that it was going to be impossible to reach a consensus, the goat, which had been positioned very close to the smelly kid, fainted.

This doesn't really fall into the category of horror stories but contemplation of the class retreat—a requirement for graduation—was regarded with horror. Despite all the big talk beforehand, everyone in our class took part to the best of my knowledge.

The retreat was conducted for us at a location about 40 miles from the city. We were bused there on a Friday afternoon and returned on a Sunday evening—about 48 hours later. A high school senior doesn't easily give up a weekend for a spiritual retreat. Especially, when the stories coming fom prior participants were sufficient to scare the wits out of everyone. It was boring, boring, boring and everyone had to go to confession—regardless of how long it had been since the last one. And that was still in the era of long litanies of sins. So a jerk who hadn't been to confession for several months could look forward to a half-hour confession at the minimum. Even if you could keep your litany of sins to 10 or 15 minutes you were sure to get a lecture of equal length.

Fortunately, the misery of uncertainty that preceeded the retreat was worse than the certain misery that prevailed during same. It was tough, though. Silence was the mandate. Talking was permitted only at specified times. Much time was spent reading or in contemplation. The only allowed reading material was religious in nature. Somehow, all survived. But barely, I think. There was a lot of yelling and screaming on the bus trip home and just hearing one of the pop songs on the radio was a real treat.

Yes, everybody did have to go to confession. It took nearly the 48 hours to get through the group of over 40. It took several weekends to put through the entire graduating class of about 225.

Graduation From High School

This was the end of formal Catholic education for many, if not most, Catholic kids. A reasonably high percentage of Catholic high school grads went on to college. While it was still discussed as to whether or not one could attend a secular college and still get to heaven, it was generally agreed that attending a secular college, a much less expensive option than attending a Catholic college was not, in itself, damaging to one's faith. If one attended the Newman Center on campus (that's before the Newman Centers went wildly liberal) salvation was still possible however statistically improbable.

So we assembled in a big church a few miles from the school for graduation. It had been a tough four years but it was over. Things probably haven't really changed that much. We wore the traditional caps and gowns and got the traditinal commencement speech.

Not much happened during the ceremony. I think we were all too happy to have it be over to use our creative juices to provide ourselves some entertainment. It was a pretty sterile ceremony. Everyone was called by his full and complete name. For example, Joseph Paul Swanson just as he was being handed his diploma. One kid had a funny middle name, a name common for a pet dog. When his name was called one of the other kids whistled as if calling a dog. It really wasn't much above a whisper and the tittering was confined to a small area.

That was about it. They just freed us into the secular world to fight anything that might damage our faith. Most of us, I strongly suspect, have been absorbed into the secular world without doing it much harm or good. In fact we probably don't even show. But we have a few characteristics that will separate us at times. And one of them is that we still don't talk in the lavatory.

DEDICATION

In memory of my father.

To my mother who encouraged me to persevere.

To my wife Sue, brothers Paul and Bill and sister Barbara who advised, edited and proofread.

To my sons Tom and Mike.

To all my friends and relatives who reminisced with me and knowingly or unknowingly helped refresh my memory.